THE
HABITS
of a
DISCIPLE

LEARNING TO WALK WITH GOD

RAY BENTLEY

THE HABITS OF A DISCIPLE
LEARNING TO WALK WITH GOD
Second Edition
by Ray Bentley

Published by

⛰ MARANATHA PRESS

© 2001, 2016 Ray Bentley
All rights reserved.

Printed in the United States of America
ISBN: 978-1-60039-165-1

For information, write to:

MARANATHA PRESS
10752 Coastwood Road, San Diego, CA. 92127.

Front Cover Design: Zach Andrews
Cover and Interior Layout: Brett Burner, Lamp Post

CONTENTS

A NEW LIFE

Learning To Walk With God

"The salvation of a single soul is more important than the production or preservation of all the epics and tragedies in the world."

–C.S. Lewis

*D*o you know that there is a party going on in heaven because of you? That's right. Jesus Himself said, *"There is joy in the presence of the angels of God over one sinner who repents"* (Luke 15:10).

Whether you have asked Jesus into your life for the first time or you are recommitting your life to Him, this is a time of great joy in heaven and a fresh beginning for you. God wants to bless you and fill you with His Spirit. He desires for you to experience the attributes of His Spirit in your own life: love, joy, peace, patience, kindness, goodness, faithfulness, gentleness, and self-control.

The Gospel of John says, *"To all who received Him, to those who believed in His name, He gave the right to become children of God—children born not out of natural descent. Nor human decision or a husband's will, but born of God"* (NIV).

In other words, you have been "born again." You are now His child and just like any loving parent, God wants to help you live life abundantly. He has a wonderful plan for your life!

What Does It Mean to Be Born Again?

One night a man named Nicodemus came to Jesus, desiring to strike up a conversation. As a respected leader in his community, Nicodemus was perhaps embarrassed to be seen with such a controversial character as Jesus, so he approached Him "after hours."

"Rabbi," Nicodemus began, "we know you are a teacher who has come from God. For no one could perform the miraculous signs you are doing if God were not with him." Nicodemus acknowledged Jesus as a good teacher and even as someone capable of miracles. Jesus recognized a man hungering for the truth, so He didn't waste any time with philosophical discussions or polite conversation. He got right to the point: *"I tell you the truth, unless a man is born again, he cannot see the kingdom of God"* (John 3:3).

This is the first time in recorded history that this now-common phrase, "born again," was used. Nicodemus was baffled, and asked Jesus, skeptically, "How can a man be born when he is old? Surely he cannot enter a second time into his mother's womb to be born!"

So Jesus explained it to him this way: "Unless a man is born of water and the Spirit, he cannot enter the kingdom of God. Flesh gives birth to flesh, but the Spirit gives birth to spirit."

Nicodemus' mind was reeling as he tried to think this through. Even with all his knowledge and intellectual prowess, he was still confused as he blurted out, "How can this be?"

Jesus gently chided him, saying, "Are you a teacher of Israel and still do not know these things?"

In other words, whether you are brand new to spiritual things, or a very religious person—perhaps even a leader in your church or temple—you can still be ignorant or confused about the one essential condition stipulated by Jesus for entering the Kingdom of God.

It's actually quite logical, when you think about how Jesus explained it. "Flesh gives birth to flesh." The five billion people on planet earth got here one way—and one way only. Each of us came from our mother's womb.

There is another, spiritual, invisible world, all around us, inhabited by spiritual beings, like angels, and ruled by a loving, caring, and benevolent God, creator of the universe. There is only one way to enter this world as well. "That which is born of the Spirit is spirit," Jesus said. You must be spiritually born into it. You must be born again, by the Spirit of God.

The Spirit is like the wind, Jesus explained. We cannot physically see the Spirit of God. But just as we can "see" the wind blowing in tree tops and feel its breeze upon our faces, we can feel and see the effects of God's Spirit in our lives.

After Jesus and Nicodemus met, Jesus soon got to the very heart of what all this means: *"For God so loved the world that He gave His one and only Son, that whoever believes in Him shall not perish but have eternal life"* (John 3:16).

That's what it means to be born again. By the Holy Spirit of God, we have the opportunity to pass from death to life. We are no longer bound by this world and its constraints. We will not perish. Our sin, our pain, our misery, the heartaches and failures that torment and taunt us are now subject to a new order, a new way of thinking and living—a new, eternal life in the Kingdom of God!

A New Start

Do you ever wake up in the morning and resolve—once again—to fix whatever's wrong in your life? Sometimes it feels like—if we could just get a new house…or job…or wife…or husband…then all our problems would go away. We promise to lose weight, eat better, work harder, work less, etc., etc. Do you ever wish you could just start over?

We get that chance the moment we are born again.

From the minute we are physically born, God's spirit is with us. That's why we are so very aware of Him. Most people have a religious understanding and even an historical acceptance of His existence. But believing in Him and knowing Him is a different matter.

Jesus says, in the book of Revelation, "Behold I stand at the door and knock." He desires that we open the door to our hearts and allow Him to come in. He longs to have a relationship with us. But all of us are separated, by nature, from God by our sins. *"All have sinned and fall short of the glory of God,"* says the Bible (Romans 3:23).

The good news is that when we ask Jesus into our lives, He begins to transform us. *"Therefore, if anyone is in Christ, he is a new creature; old things have passed away; behold all things have become new,"* says 2 Corinthians 5:17.

He gives us a chance to start over, to be renewed by His Spirit, to literally be born again. And the process doesn't stop there. He continues to change us and bless us until we reach our final destination in heaven.

"But we all...are being transformed...from glory to glory, by the spirit of the Lord" (2 Corinthians 3:18).

"He who has begun a good work in you will complete it until the day of Christ Jesus" (Philippians 1:6).

A First Step

Just as a baby is first conceived, then grows inside its mother's womb before being born, the concept of a relationship with God begins with a tiny seed of thought or recognition of a need in our lives. We long to know what life is really about.

Jesus taught, *"It is the spirit who gives life; the flesh profits nothing. The words that I speak to you are spirit, and they are life"* (John 6:63).

He also said, *"He who hears My Word and believes... shall not come into judgment, but has passed from death to life"* (John 5:24).

Life! By believing what Jesus taught and receiving Him into your life, you are born again into a new life! The Bible says, *"But as many as receive Him, to them He gave the right to become children of God..."* (John 1:12).

You can receive Jesus into your life and become a child of God by simply asking. Ask Him to:

1. *Help you recognize your spiritual need and to acknowledge your sins.*

2. *To forgive you of your sins.*
3. *To come into your life.*
4. *To fill you with His Spirit, helping you to walk with Him daily.*

Then pray, out of the sincerity of your heart, your own version of this simple prayer:

Dear Lord,

I know I am a sinner. I am so sorry for all the things I've done to hurt others and to break Your heart. I believe that You died to save me from my sin and I ask You to help me change. I open the door to my heart and my life and ask You to come in as my Lord and Savior. Thank you for loving me and saving me. Amen.

Should I Get Baptized?

Baptism is an outward sign of what has happened to you on the inside. Think of it like a wedding ceremony. People get married publicly to declare their love and commitment to one another before God and family and friends. Baptism is like that—a public commitment to Jesus. Like a wedding, it can also be a time of joy and fellowship as other believers encourage you in your faith.

Baptism also symbolizes the death of our old life, the burial of our sins in a watery grave, and the beginning of a new life in Jesus. The Bible says we are *"buried with Him in baptism, and raised with Him through your faith in the power of God, who raised Him from the dead"* (Colossians 2:12).

Growing Up in Christ

Being born again is literally like starting over as a spiritual infant. In the joy and excitement of knowing Jesus, sometimes we are in a hurry to "grow up." But the secret to spiritual maturity is that it takes time. It's a learning process. There are no shortcuts to spiritual growth, no magic pill. Having an emotional experience does not automatically make any of us spiritual giants.

This is good news. God knows that a new believer is like a precious infant who needs to be nurtured and taught. He is patient even if we aren't.

Believers are called "disciples" because we are learning new disciplines—or habits—in our lives. The more we apply these disciplines to our lives, the more we grow and can be used by God.

Have you ever noticed that it is easier to form good habits than it is to get rid of bad habits? The best way to get rid of bad habits is to replace them with good ones. So part of our goal in this little book is to help you form new, godly disciplines that will enrich your life and draw you closer to the Lord. Take some time to study each section and apply it personally to your life as we examine the habits of a disciple of Christ.

I'd like to note, with appreciation, that some of the points listed under each section came from a discipleship series taught by Pastor Rick Warren.

THE POWER OF GOD'S WORD

"All the good from the Savior of the world is communicated through this Book. All the things desirable to man are contained in it."
                                                    —Abraham Lincoln

*W*hile it is vitally important for you to be involved in a good church that teaches from the Bible, it is equally important for you to study God's Word for yourself. You've heard the saying, "If you give a man a fish, you've fed him for a meal. But if you teach a man to fish, you've fed him for a lifetime." I want to teach you to feed yourself.

Hear the Word

The easiest way to get into God's Word is to hear it. "Consequently, faith comes from hearing the message, and the message is heard through the word of Christ," the Bible says (Romans 10:17, NIV). Listening to God's Word increases your faith and allows you to hear Him speak. Sermon archives, Bible apps, internet sites and resources, radio, and televised services are all sources for hearing God's Word. There are a couple of problems, however.

Statistically, we tend to forget 95% of what we hear within 72 hours. That's why people can go to church week after week, year after year, and not really grow spiritually. How can you apply what you hear if you don't remember it? Here are some ways to improve your hearing:

- **Be eager to hear what God has to say to you.** Listen to the Word, expecting God to speak directly to you. *"How sweet are your words to my taste, sweeter than honey to my mouth!"* the Psalmist wrote (Psalm 119:103).

- **Confess any sin in your life.** Don't be afraid to talk to God about your failures, weaknesses and everything you know is not pleasing to Him. *"Lay aside all filthiness and overflow of wickedness, and receive with meekness the* *implanted Word, which is able to save your souls"* (James 1:21).

- **Takes notes!** The act of writing down what you hear increases your chance of remembering it and reviewing. *"We must pay more careful attention, therefore, to what we have heard, so that we do not drift away"* (Hebrews 2:1, NIV).

- **Act on what you hear.** *"Do not merely listen to the Word, and so deceive yourself. Do what it says...The man who looks intently into the perfect law that gives freedom, and continues to do this, not forgetting what he has heard, but doing it—he will be blessed in what he does"* (James 1:22-25, NIV).

Read the Word

The other problem with only hearing the Word is that you are still dependent on someone else to feed you, whatever the media. Reading you can do by yourself, with the aid of the Holy Spirit, *"whom the Father will send in My name,"* Jesus said, *"[and] He will teach you all things..."* (John 14:26).

The ancient Hebrews taught, *"That copy of the laws shall be his constant companion. He must read from it every day of his life so that he will learn to respect the Lord his God by obeying all of his commands"* (Deuteronomy 17:19, TLB).

Reading the Word everyday is a way of spiritually feeding yourself, preventing spiritual malnourishment. Reading the Word daily also draws you closer to God, helping to build that close, intimate relationship He desires to have with you.

If you are new to reading the Bible or even if you are starting over, I suggest that you start with the Gospels. Read through them systematically, for at least fifteen minutes a day. Read out loud if it helps you focus; read at night, first thing in the morning, or whenever you just feel spiritually hungry.

If you read nothing else in your whole life, read through the Bible. You'll not only discover a great piece of literature, rich in human drama and poetry, but also the source of Truth and the Words of God Himself.

Study the Word

First you hear the Word, then you read the Word. Now it's time to study the Word, to dig deep and really get to know the depth of the Bible's wisdom and truth and how they apply to your life.

"Be diligent to present yourself approved to God, a worker who does not need to be ashamed, rightly dividing the word of truth," wrote the apostle Paul, from his prison cell, to his young friend, Timothy (2 Timothy 2:15). Paul

understood how important it was for Timothy to "rightly divide the truth," by studying the Scriptures. Each of us needs to do the same.

Begin to build a good study library, starting with a study Bible such as: the Life Application Bible, Ryrie Study Bible, Thompson Chain Reference, Scofield Bible, Vine's Expository Reference Bible or the Open Bible, to name a few.

Study helps such as Halley's Bible Handbook, Strong's Exhaustive Concordance, The New Bible Dictionary (Eerdmans), the Moody Atlas of Bible Lands and one of the many "read-through-the-Bible-in-a-year" reading plans are good. All these and numerous other sources are available online.

Memorize the Word

"Keep my Words and live, and my law as the apple of your eye. Bind them on your fingers; write them on the tablet of your heart," the Lord advised his people, and with good reason (Proverbs 7:2-3).

There is power in memorizing God's Word! If you don't think you can memorize anything, realize that most of us can recite TV commercials or baseball scores or recipes or jokes without even thinking. We've committed to memory the things that interest us and surround us. I'm amazed at the amount of trivia that fills my brain. And for what?

Memorizing God's Word, on the other hand, produces enormous benefits. Such as:

- **God's Word will help us resist temptation.** *"I have hidden Your Word in my heart that I might not sin against You"* (Psalm 119:11, NIV).

- **God's Word helps us make wise decisions.** *"Your Word is a lamp to my feet and a light to my path"* (Psalm 119:105).

- **God's Word strengthens us when we're under stress.** *"My comfort in my suffering is this: Your promise preserves my life"* (Psalm 119:50).

- **God's Word comforts us when we're discouraged.** *"Your Word was to me the joy and rejoicing of my heart"* (Jeremiah 15:16).

- **God's Word helps us share our faith with others.** *"Always be prepared to give the reason for the hope that you have…"* (1 Peter 3:15).

Meditate

As you listen, read, study and memorize God's Word, there is one more step—perhaps the most important one—to being able to apply what you've learned to your life: meditate (or contemplate). Meditation is simply focused thinking about a particular passage of Scripture, to discover how you can best apply its truth to your life. The word meditate is related to the word ruminate, which refers to the idea of a cow chewing its cud.

Do you know that a cow has eight stomachs, and each piece of grass that a cow swallows has to go through each stomach and be re-chewed each time? That may sound a little unappetizing, but think about how well-digested that grass is by the time the cow is done.

So it is when we ruminate on a morsel of truth.

Taking the time to contemplate God's Word helps us in many ways, including:

- **It helps us to change.** *"Be transformed by the renewing of your mind,"* says Romans 12:2. Your life is shaped by your thoughts. The truth is that we become whatever we think about the most. Contemplating the Lord and His Word helps us to be more like Him.

- **It is the key to answered prayer.** *"If you remain in Me and My words remain in you, ask whatever you wish and it will be given you"* (John 15:7).

- **It is the key to a successful life.** *"This book of the law shall not depart from your mouth, but you shall meditate on it day and night, that you may* *observe to do according to all that is written in it. For then you will make your way prosperous, and then you shall have good success"* (Joshua 1:8).

THE POWER
OF PRAYER

"Prayer enlarges the heart until it is capable of containing God's gift of Himself."
                                                        –Mother Teresa

Psalm 42 has a wonderful passage in which the psalmist cries out to God, *"Deep calls unto deep... the Lord will command His lovingkindness in the daytime, and in the night His song shall be with me—a prayer to the God of my life."*

When God's Spirit touches the deepest part of our souls, we can respond by acknowledging Him, and answering Him through prayer.

Prayer is a spiritual way of describing how we talk with God. It is the way we humans can respond to God as He calls us to come to Him. In the book of Genesis, where we read about Adam and Eve sinning and hiding from the presence of God, we also read that *"the Lord God called to Adam and said to him, 'Where are you?'"* (Genesis 3:9).

God continues to call out to each of His children, every day, drawing us close to Him, wanting us to realize that He truly is just a prayer away.

Prayer will allow you to experience intimacy with God. *"Call to me,"* the Lord says in Jeremiah 33:3, "and I will answer you, and show you great and mighty things which you do not know."

In prayer we get a taste of eternal life, when we will know God intimately. Prayer is not a time to learn or study more about God, but instead, is time spent with God. Prayer allows you to become aware of the strength and love imparted to us by the miraculous presence of God's Holy Spirit in our lives.

Pray Everyday

When a crisis hits, we humans are quick to pray. Nothing wrong with that! "God! Help!" is a legitimate prayer. But we were made for more than that. We were created by God to be in His presence every day. He enjoys and de-sires our company. *"Look!"* Jesus said. *"I've been standing at the door constantly knocking. If anyone...opens the door, I will come in and fellowship with him and he with me"* (Revelation 3:20, Living Bible).

Jesus literally died to make it possible for us to have a relationship with God.

When Adam and Eve sinned, mankind's fellowship with God was broken—and, amazingly, God had a problem. His holiness and purity could not be compromised. On the other hand, He created us for fellowship and intimacy with Him. How to bridge the gap between absolute holiness and our sinful nature? *"But God demonstrates His own love toward us, in that while we were still sinners, Christ died for us"* (Romans 5:8).

Jesus knew the importance of daily prayer. He drew strength from the time He spent alone with His heavenly Father. He often withdrew from the mainstream of busy life to pray, setting an example for us. We cannot be healthy Christians without time spent in prayer.

How to Begin A Daily Prayer Time

Again, Jesus set the example for us. The Gospel of Mark tells us, *"Now in the morning, having risen a long while before daylight, He went out and departed to a solitary place; and there He prayed"* (Mark 1:35).

Do you have to be up before daylight? Or hike out to a solitary desert spot? Or be there for hours? No! The point is, Jesus found a time and a place when and where

He could be alone with His heavenly Father. Morning is good for a lot of people because that is when they are at their best, but you need to pick a time that works for you.

I suggest starting with 15 minutes each day, because, like exercise, if you start with too much and find you can't keep it up, you'll get discouraged and quit. Start with 15 minutes and grow from there. When time with the Lord is a priority, your heart will hunger for more, as your relationship with Him grows deeper, more intimate. Ultimately, the Bible says, we are to *"pray without ceasing,"* (I Thessalonians 5:17) as we learn to seek God at every turn and realize the enormous benefits of daily prayer.

The Purpose of Prayer

Prayer strengthens us and enables us to:

- **Worship God**

  "Give unto the Lord the glory due His name; worship the Lord in the beauty of holiness" (Psalm 29:2).

- **Receive direction from God**

  "Trust in the Lord with all your heart, and lean not on your own understanding; in all your ways acknowledge Him and He shall direct your paths" (Proverbs 3:5-6).

- **Be filled with joy**

  "Delight yourself also in the Lord, and He shall give you the desires of your heart" (Psalm 37:4).

How to Pray

I said earlier that prayer is simply talking with God. Prayer also sustains us through those tough times in life. As the apostle Paul wrote to the believers of his time: *"Base your happiness on your hope in Christ. When trials come endure them patiently; steadfastly maintain the habit of prayer"* (Romans 12:12, Phillips translation). When you read through the Scriptures, from Genesis to Revelation, you'll find men and women who spoke to God with honesty, boldness and from their hearts.

For those of us who feel intimidated by the prospect of talking to the Creator of the universe, or who don't know where or how to begin, Jesus gave us a model prayer to get us started.

The Lord's Prayer has been recited in Congress, Sunday schools and prayer meetings for centuries. As we take a closer look at it, we'll see how each portion of this famous prayer draws us deeper into a relationship with the living God. Rick Warren breaks the Lord's Prayer down into six elements, through which can appreciate the depth and scope of Jesus' prayer.

The disciples had come to Jesus and simply requested, "Lord, teach us to pray." Jesus responded, telling them to pray this way:

> *Our Father in heaven,*
> *Hallowed be Your name.*

Your kingdom come,
Your will be done
On earth as it is in heaven.
Give us this day our daily bread.
And forgive us our sins,
For we also forgive everyone who is indebted to us.
And do not lead us into temptation,
But deliver us from the evil one.

Luke 11:2-4, NKJV

Praise

"Our Father in heaven, hallowed be Your name."

Jesus taught His disciples to pray by focusing, not on themselves or their needs, but on God. He taught them to honor God and to praise Him for Who He is. If we come to prayer more focused on ourselves than on the Lord, I guarantee we'll leave our prayer time more depressed and frustrated than when we began.

God asks us to look up, to see Him, to lift our eyes above the circumstances of this world. *"Enter in His gates with thanksgiving, and into His courts with praise. Be thankful to Him and bless His name"* (Psalm 100:4).

You might be asking yourself, how can I sincerely praise God for who He is when I really don't know yet? That's where time in the Word comes in. You discover God's character by reading His Word, and as you do, you will discover what the prophet Nehemiah learned:

"You are a forgiving God, gracious and compassion ate, slow to anger and abounding in love" (Nehemiah 9:17, NIV).

Part of praise is thankfulness. "Those who thank God much are the truly wealthy," said Albert Schweitzer. Our whole attitude toward life will change when you begin to thank God for what's good, for what you learn everyday, and mostly, for His love.

Purpose

"Your kingdom come, Your will be done, on earth as it is in heaven."

When I originally taught this message at our church, I carefully explained why God's will is always best for our lives, and leads to blessing. The opposite of God's blessings is our will, which usually leads to disaster. I summed up this serious thought with, "You are no longer the boss of the applesauce."

Where there had been some tears over the joy of newfound salvation, I now saw incredulous looks in the eyes of those who were listening. The boss of what? I tried to recover by blaming it on my wife and her Midwest sayings, but it didn't matter. God had greater things in mind than my pastoral dignity. The point is, we need to acknowledge that God is God—and we're not. Our total surrender to His will always leads to a richer, fuller life.

"Therefore, I urge you, brothers, in view of God's mercy, to offer your bodies as living sacrifices, holy and pleasing to God—which is your spiritual worship" (Romans 12:1, NIV).

Provision
"Give us this day our daily bread."

Jesus taught His disciples to ask God to provide for our needs. What needs? Anything and everything! Whatever bothers you touches the heart of God. Whatever needs you have are His concern.

"And my God will meet all your needs according to His glorious riches in Christ Jesus" (Philippians 4:19, NIV).

"He who did not spare His own Son, but gave Him up for us all—how will he not also, along with Him, graciously give us all things?" (Romans 8:32, NIV).

"You do not have, because you not ask God" (James 4:2), NIV).

Pardon
"And forgive us our sins…"

Billy Graham once said, "If His conditions are met, God is bound by His Word to forgive any man or any woman of any sin because of Christ." The conditions we need to meet begin with the simple line above. "Forgive us our sins."

If you're not sure how to begin to ask for forgiveness, here are some suggestions:

- **Ask the Holy Spirit to reveal sin in your life.**

  "Search me, O God, and know my heart: try me, and know my thoughts and see if there be any wicked way in me, and lead me in the way everlasting" (Psalm 139: 23-24).

- **Confess each sin.**

  Rather than just gloss over a general list, be honest with yourself. Take a personal inventory of the areas of your life that need to be dealt with.

  "He who covers his sins will not prosper, but whoever confesses and forsakes them will have mercy" (Proverbs 28:13).

- **Make restitution to others when necessary.**

  Don't allow old grudges, family quarrels or wounds you have inflicted to go unresolved.

  "If you bring a gift to the altar, and there remember that your brother has something against you, leave your gift there before the altar and go your way. First be reconciled to your brother, and then come and offer your gift" (Matthew 5:23-24).

- **Receive God's forgiveness.**

  "Where is the foolish person who thinks it in his power to commit more than God could forgive?" wrote a sixteenth century monk. He was right. There is nothing you have done that cannot be forgiven. And the first step toward changing your life is to acknowledge your need for forgiveness, then accept what God has promised:

"If we confess our sins, He is faithful and just and will forgive our sins and purify us from all unrighteousness" (1 John 1:9).

Pardon Others

"For we also forgive everyone who is indebted to us."

Forgiveness can be hard. Letting go of hurts and resentments can be painful and nearly impossible. But "with God all things are possible." In His Word, I've discovered three keys to unlocking forgiveness:

- **Understanding**

  "As a father has compassion on his children, so the Lord has compassion on those who fear Him; for He knows how we are formed, He remembers that we are dust" (Psalm 103:13-14).

- **Forgetting**

  "For I will forgive their wickedness and will remember their sin no more" (Jeremiah 31:34, NIV).

- **Love**

  "Love is patient, love is kind. It does not envy, it does not boast, it is not proud. It is not rude, it is not self-seeking, it is not easily

angered, it keeps no record of wrongs. Love does not delight in evil but rejoices with truth. It always protects, always trusts, always hopes, always preserves. Love never fails" (1 Corinthians 13:4-8, NIV).

Protection

"And do not lead us into temptation, but deliver us from the evil one."

As believers, we face a spiritual battle every day of our lives. Fear and temptation are constant foes, inflicted on us by the enemy of our souls, Satan. By praying for the Lord's protection every day, we can have the confidence to face any situation that comes our way.

"You are children of God, little children, and have overcome them, because He who is in you is greater than he who is in the world" (1 John 4:4).

"But seek first His kingdom and His righteousness, and all these things will be given to you as well. Therefore do not worry about tomorrow, for tomorrow will worry about itself. Each day has enough trouble of its own" (Matthew 6:33-34, NIV).

My prayer for you is that prayer will be a priority in your life. Not a duty or a religious activity, but time spent in God's presence, drawing you close to Him, allowing His Spirit to enrich you, encourage you and empower you to live a victorious life in Christ.

THE HABIT OF FELLOWSHIP

"We are all strings in the concert of His joy." —Jacob Boehme

*F*ellowship a habit? Isn't that just hanging out with other Christians or going to church? Yes, but it's that and so much more. And yes, fellowship should become a habit in your life.

Why?

Because we need each other to grow spiritually.

Charles Spurgeon, the great evangelist of the nineteenth century, told the story of a woman who came to him claiming that her relationship with God was just fine, even though she saw no need to actually attend church. As she chattered away, he walked over to the fireplace in the room, and with the tongs, picked out a blazing coal. He carefully set the coal on the hearth, all the while listening as she made her case. She noted his actions but failed to see their significance until he asked her to observe the coal. The once red-hot coal, separated from the warmth of the fire, grew colder and colder, sitting alone on the hearth.

The significance of the lonely coal was not lost on his friend. *"As iron sharpens iron, so a man sharpens the countenance of a friend,"* says the book of Proverbs (27:17) in the Old Testament of the Bible. Encouragement, discussion, accountability and soul searching with other believers help us mature as Christians. Constructive critiquing can be a valuable gift between two friends. *"But encourage one another daily, as long as it is called today, so that none of you may be hardened by sin's deceitfulness"* (Hebrews 3:13).

- **Fellowship is important because we are members of the same family.** God's family! You can't build a strong family unless its members spend time with one another. Families help each other in times of hardship, and rejoice together in times of blessing.

  "Let us not give up meeting together, as some are in the habit of doing, but let us encourage one another" (Hebrews 10:25, NIV).

"Therefore, as we have opportunity, let us do good to all people, especially to those who belong to the family of believers" (Galatians 6:10).

- **The Bible promises us that Jesus is present and His power is manifested when we pray together.**

  "Again I say to you that if two of you agree on earth concerning anything that they ask, it will be done for them by My father in heaven. For where two or three are gathered together in My name, I am there in the midst of them" (Matthew 18:19,20).

- **Fellowship shares the good news of God's love to the world.**

  Jesus said, *"By this shall all men know that you are my disciples, if you have love for one another"* (John 13:35).

  Like family members, Christians all too often squabble, gossip and even persecute one another – not quite what Jesus had in mind when He said to "love one another." Loving, caring and ministering to each other makes a statement to the world about the truth of the Gospel.

- **We are indebted to every other believer.**

  In a sense, we owe other believers our talents and gifts. The apostle Peter taught, *"Each one should use whatever gifts he has received to serve others, faithfully administering God's grace in its various forms"* (1 Peter 4:10).

The Lord put us together to bless one another, complement one another and to see our gifts and talents blossom and be used. "Various forms," Peters said. That means we are not given the same gifts. Some may be gifted in the arts like writing or music or art. Others in administration or childcare, or counseling or teaching or construction or cooking...the list is endless. When we become part of the church through our faith in Jesus, we are not only on the receiving end of the others' gifts, but we also get the opportunity to use our gifts to bless others.

Don't ever run away from the love, support and encouragement that being part of a church can give you. Christians are not perfect people. You can find lots of things to criticize in any church, if you choose. But the truth of God is not changed—not one iota—by the failings of people. He loves you and wants you to be blessed through His body of believers, by giving and receiving.

Large church or small church?

There are two types of church meetings: large and small. In the early church days, people met in homes. But one of the first church services, as recorded in the book Acts, had over 3000 in attendance! Jesus taught His disciples in a small group of twelve, but He also spoke to masses of people, like the day He taught the Sermon on the Mount. Both large and small gatherings of believers are good.

The important thing is, we are taught that we need one another. Take some time to look up all the "one another" passages in the Bible and you'll see the importance of fellowship in your life.

If you attend a large church, find a small group within that church in which you can develop close and spiritual friendships. I've seen home fellowships in our church knit together by life long friendships; people who come to love each other as brothers and sisters. They rejoice at weddings and births and graduations, and care for one another during hard and sad times. They fulfill the "one anothers" in the Bible.

"When God's children are in need, be the one to help them out. And get into the habit of inviting guests home for dinner, or, if they need lodging, for the night" (Romans 12:13, NLT).

SHARING YOUR FAITH

"He who can tell men what God has done for his soul is the likeliest to bring their souls to God." —Robert Leighton

Have you ever heard of the San Andreas Fault? This notorious earthquake fault, which runs through California and keeps people waiting in anticipation for the "big one," which was named after Jesus' friend and disciple, Andrew. Compared to his brother Peter, Andrew was a relatively unknown, quiet, yet deep man. Not much action on the surface, but when he acted, something happened. Just like his geological namesake.

Andrew is brought to center stage only three times in the Gospels. And in all three instances, he is seen bringing people to Jesus. (Read John 1:40-42, John 6:8-9, 12:21-22.)

Andrew dedicated his life to sharing the friendship and loving relationship he experienced with the Lord, with others. Andrew was a true friend. "To love another person is to help them love God," said Søren Kierkegaard.

In the book of John, chapter one, verse 38, Jesus turned to a group of men walking behind Him and asked, "What do you seek?" That is the question God is asking each of us—everyone on this planet is seeking something. We all desire in some way to understand the meaning of our lives, why we are here, what we are supposed to do. Everyone you love and care about faces the same questions. What better gift can you offer them than to do as Andrew did and point them toward the Giver of life, Jesus, who proclaimed, "I am the Way, the Truth and the Life"?

That is why we often ask people to get up and walk forward during our church service to publicly confess their new faith in Christ. It is the first step in allowing God to give you the courage to share your faith.

It's not always easy to know what to say, to speak up to friends, neighbors, co-workers, and family. The best advice I can give you is: pray, read the Word, be in fellowship with other believers—and then pray some more! All the things we've discussed, which will help you to grow in Christ, will cause your faith and love for God to overflow and spill out to other people. Let your witnessing be led by the Spirit, and the love God gives you for others.

"But in your hearts set apart Christ as Lord. Always be prepared to give the reason for the hope that you have. But do this with gentleness and respect…" (1 Peter 3: 15-16, NIV).

"Go to all the world and preach the gospel to every creature" (Jesus' words, Mark 16:15).

The Money Question—the Habit of Tithing

Finally we come to an issue that probably stumbles more people and gives non-believers an excuse to stay away from "religion" than just about anything.

Money.

Before I go any further, let me say without reservation: God does not need your money! Neither His love for us, the work of His Spirit in our world, or the existence of His church depend on our money. So, if anyone ever tries to tell you they do, direct them to God's Word. The Psalms declare that God owns the cattle on a thousand hills! *"The world is Mine and all its fullness,"* He said (Psalm 50:10-12).

So why do we talk about tithes and offerings?

Because part of our spiritual growth depends on our ability to realize where our blessings come from and to be able to freely give to others, sharing our material blessings. It is freeing to not be hung up about hoarding our money, but to be able to be wise with it, and in the process, learn to give liberally.

God set the example for us by giving freely to us—everything. *"For God so loved the world that He gave his only begotten Son, that whoever believes in Him should not perish but have everlasting life"* (John 3:16). He gave us life, light, love, warmth, food and everything that is good! He gives us the gift of eternal life. Giving is part of God's nature, and therefore, will become part of ours when we follow Him.

The word "tithe" means "a tenth part." The guidelines given in Scripture are that we should give, or "tithe," ten percent of our incomes back to the Lord. Why? The Bible gives the following reasons:

- **Because God commands it.**

  He told the children of Israel, *"A tenth of all you produce is the Lord's, and it is holy"* (Leviticus 27:30).

- **Because Jesus commends it.**

  Tithing was not just an Old Testament law. Jesus also strongly encouraged believers to give, but with this strong exhortation: *"Woe upon you, Pharisees and you religious leaders—hypocrites! For you tithe down to the last mint leaf in your garden, but ignore the important things—justice and mercy and faith. Yes, you should tithe, but don't leave the more important things undone"* (Matthew 23:23, Living Bible).

- **Tithing demonstrates that God has first place in my life.**

  "The purpose of tithing is to teach you to always put God first in your lives," says Deuteronomy 14:23 (Living Bible). When you can let go of the fear of giving—and it is a fear, of not being able to have enough or keep enough—then you are exercising your faith by completely trusting the Lord with your life, including your finances.

- **Tithing reminds me that everything was given to me by God.**

  "But remember the Lord your God, for it is He who gives you the ability to produce wealth" (Deuteronomy 8:18, NIV).

- **Tithing expresses my gratitude.**

  "How can I repay the Lord for all His goodness to me?" the Psalmist asked (Psalm 116:12). The answer is, you can't. But you can demonstrate your gratefulness with your generosity and trust in His provision.

- **God says that refusing to tithe is like robbing Him.**

That's kind of a hard concept to swallow, but this is what the Bible says:

"Will a man rob God? Yet you rob Me.

"But, you ask, 'How do we rob you?'

"In tithes and offerings. You are under a curse—the whole nation of you—because you are robbing me" (Malachi 3:8-9).

The other side of this is what God wants to do for us when we do tithe:

- **Tithing gives God a chance to prove He exists and wants to bless you.**

  "Bring the whole tithe into the storehouse, that there may be food in my house. 'Test me in this,' says the Lord Almighty, 'and see if I will not throw open the floodgates of heaven and pour out so much blessing that you will not have room enough for it" (Malachi 3:10, NIV).

I believe this is the only time in the Bible that God says, "test me." He not only wants to prove to us that He exists, but He also desires to pour out blessings in abundance.

- **Tithing gives us an opportunity to express our love for God through obedience.**

  "If you love me, you will obey what I command" (John 14:15, NIV).

One last thought on tithing. The Bible tells us that God loves a cheerful giver (2 Corinthians 9:7). His Word promises right after that verse, "God is able to make all grace abound toward you." He never wants us to give grudgingly, or fearfully. But if it is hard for you to give "cheerfully," then pray and ask Him for a heart that desires to give and to bless others.

As you begin your new life in Christ, my prayer is that you will grow in the grace and knowledge of God and that you will experience the reality of the *"love of God poured out into our hearts by the Holy Spirit"* (Romans 5:5).

We've included the Gospel of John plus a daily reading schedule with this book to get you started. It would be our joy and privilege to encourage you and pray for you in your walk with the Lord.

You may contact us through our webpage at:
www.maranathachapel.org

May God richly bless you!

THE GOSPEL OF JOHN

of

JOHN

TWENTY-ONE DAYS WITH GOD

TWENTY-ONE DAYS WITH GOD

As a first step in your journey toward developing the habits of a disciple, we encourage you to begin by reading a chapter a day in the Gospel of John.

Written by John—the son of Zebedee and Salome, the brother of James, a Galilean fisherman, and finally, an apostle of Jesus Christ—this fourth book of the New Testament is often called "God's Love Letter."

John wrote this account of his life with Jesus after his fellow apostles had died and gone to be with the Lord. John's is the most spiritual of the Gospels, and explores in depth the meanings of the Incarnation and the love of God. John also introduces the doctrine of the Holy Spirit as the Comforter.

John wrote from his heart, with a longing to impress upon his readers the words of life and love that had so deeply affected his own life. He summed up his purpose for writing this book saying,*"These are written that you might believe that Jesus is the Christ, the Son of God, and that believing you may have life in His name"* (John 20:31).

As you begin reading the Gospel of John each day, pray and ask the Lord to speak to you through His Word. Then, expect Him to minister to you, looking for:

1. A Promise to Claim
2. Something to Enrich your Life
3. Something to Change

The Bible assures us that something good will come of time spent in the Word:

"All Scripture is given by inspiration of God, and is profitable for doctrine, for reproof, for correction, for instruction in righteousness, that the man of God may be complete, thoroughly equipped for every good work" (2 Timothy 3:16-17).

By the time you finish reading John, you will have begun to develop the habit of daily time in God's Word, and it will make itself at home in your heart. I can hardly begin to tell you how this will affect you, and the power that the Lord will have in your life as you meet with Him each day.

After a while, you will naturally begin to grow and change: *"But we all, with unveiled face, beholding as in a mirror the glory of the Lord are being transformed into the same image from glory to glory, just as by the Spirit of the Lord"* (II Corinthians 3:18).

As the Lord speaks to you through His word, make a note of what He has told you that day and be encouraged that *"He delights in unchanging love"* (Micah 7:18), that *"His compassion is new every morning"* (Lamentations 3:22,23), and that He longs to *"be gracious to you"* (Isaiah 30:18).

May God bless you as you learn to walk with Him!

THE
GOSPEL *of* JOHN
TWENTY-ONE DAYS WITH GOD

1 In the beginning was the Word, and the Word was with God, and the Word was God.

2 He was in the beginning with God.

3 All things were made through Him, and without Him nothing was made that was made.

4 In Him was life, and the life was the light of men.

5 And the light shines in the darkness, and the darkness did not comprehend it.

6 There was a man sent from God, whose name was John.

7 This man came for a witness, to bear witness of the Light, that all through him might believe.

8 He was not that Light, but was sent to bear witness of that Light.

9 That was the true Light which gives light to every man coming into the world.

10 He was in the world, and the world was made through Him, and the world did not know Him.

11 He came to His own, and His own did not receive Him.

12 But as many as received Him, to them He gave the right to become children of God, to those who believe in His name:

13 who were born, not of blood, nor of the will of the flesh, nor of the will of man, but of God.

14 And the Word became flesh and dwelt among us, and we beheld His glory, the glory as of the only begotten of the Father, full of grace and truth.

15 John bore witness of Him and cried out, saying, "This was He of whom I said, 'He who comes after me is preferred before me, for He was before me.'"

16 And of His fullness we have all received, and grace for grace.

17 For the law was given through Moses, but grace and truth came through Jesus Christ.

18 No one has seen God at any time. The only begotten Son, who is in the bosom of the

Father, He has declared Him.

19 Now this is the testimony of John, when the Jews sent priests and Levites from Jerusalem to ask him, "Who are you?"

20 He confessed, and did not deny, but confessed, "I am not the Christ."

21 And they asked him, "What then? Are you Elijah?" He said, "I am not." "Are you the Prophet?" And he answered, "No."

22 Then they said to him, "Who are you, that we may give an answer to those who sent us? What do you say about yourself?"

23 He said: "I am 'The voice of one crying in the wilderness: "Make straight the way of the LORD," 'as the prophet Isaiah said."

24 Now those who were sent were from the Pharisees.

25 And they asked him, saying, "Why then do you baptize if you are not the Christ, nor Elijah, nor the Prophet?"

26 John answered them, saying, "I baptize with water, but there stands One among you whom you do not know.

27 "It is He who, coming after me, is preferred before me, whose sandal strap I am not worthy to loose."

28 These things were done in Bethabara beyond the Jordan, where John was baptizing.

29 The next day John saw Jesus coming toward him, and said, "Behold! The Lamb of God who takes away the sin of the world!

30 "This is He of whom I said, 'After me comes a Man who is preferred before me, for He was before me.'

31 "I did not know Him; but that He should be revealed to Israel, therefore I came baptizing with water."

32 And John bore witness, saying, "I saw the Spirit descending from heaven like a dove, and He remained upon Him.

33 "I did not know Him, but He who sent me to baptize with water said to me, 'Upon whom you see the Spirit descending, and remaining on Him, this is He who baptizes with the Holy Spirit.'

34 "And I have seen and testified that this is the Son of God."

35 Again, the next day, John stood with two of his disciples.

36 And looking at Jesus as He walked, he said, "Behold the Lamb of God!"

37 The two disciples heard him speak, and they followed Jesus.

38 Then Jesus turned, and seeing them following, said to them, "What do you seek?" They said to Him, "Rabbi" (which is to say, when translated, Teacher), "where are You staying?"

39 He said to them, "Come and see." They came and saw where He was staying, and remained with Him that day (now it was about the tenth hour).

40 One of the two who heard John speak, and followed Him, was Andrew, Simon Peter's brother.

41 He first found his own brother Simon, and said to him, "We have found the Messiah" (which is translated, the Christ).

42 And he brought him to Jesus. Now when Jesus looked at him, He said, "You are Simon the son of Jonah. You shall be called Cephas" (which is translated, A Stone).

43 The following day Jesus wanted to go to Galilee, and He found Philip and said to him, "Follow Me."

44 Now Philip was from Bethsaida, the city of Andrew and Peter.

45 Philip found Nathanael and said to him, "We have found Him of whom Moses in the law, and also the prophets, wrote; Jesus of Nazareth, the son of Joseph."

46 And Nathanael said to him, "Can anything good come out of Nazareth?" Philip said to him, "Come and see."

47 Jesus saw Nathanael coming toward Him, and said of him, "Behold, an Israelite indeed, in whom is no deceit!"

48 Nathanael said to Him, "How do You know me?" Jesus answered and said to him, "Before Philip called you, when you were under the fig tree, I saw you."

49 Nathanael answered and said to Him, "Rabbi, You are the Son of God! You are the King of Israel!"

50 Jesus answered and said to him, "Because I said to you, 'I saw you under the fig tree,' do you believe? You will see greater things than these."

51 And He said to him, "Most assuredly, I say to you, hereafter you shall see heaven open, and the angels of God ascending and descending upon the Son of Man."

Promise to Claim: _____

_____

_____

_____

Something to Enrich my Life:_____

_____

_____

_____

Something to Change: _____

_____

_____

_____

2 On the third day there was a wedding in Cana of Galilee, and the mother of Jesus was there.

2 Now both Jesus and His disciples were invited to the wedding.

3 And when they ran out of wine, the mother of Jesus said to Him, "They have no wine."

4 Jesus said to her, "Woman, what does your concern have to do with Me? My hour has not yet come."

5 His mother said to the servants, "Whatever He says to you, do it."

6 Now there were set there six waterpots of stone, according to the manner of purification of the Jews, containing twenty or thirty gallons apiece.

7 Jesus said to them, "Fill the waterpots with water." And they filled them up to the brim.

8 And He said to them, "Draw some out now, and take it to the master of the feast." And they took it.

9 When the master of the feast had tasted the water that was made wine, and did not know where it came from (but the servants who had drawn the water knew), the master of the feast called the bridegroom.

10 And he said to him, "Every man at the beginning sets out the good wine, and when the guests have well drunk, then the inferior. You have kept the good wine until now!"

11 This beginning of signs Jesus did in Cana of Galilee, and manifested His glory; and His disciples believed in Him.

12 After this He went down to Capernaum, He, His mother, His brothers, and His disciples; and they did not stay there many days.

13 Now the Passover of the Jews was at hand, and Jesus went up to Jerusalem.

14 And He found in the temple those who sold oxen and sheep and doves, and the

moneychangers doing business.

15 When He had made a whip of cords, He drove them all out of the temple, with the sheep and the oxen, and poured out the changers' money and overturned the tables.

16 And He said to those who sold doves, "Take these things away! Do not make My Father's house a house of merchandise!"

17 Then His disciples remembered that it was written, "Zeal for Your house has eaten Me up."

18 So the Jews answered and said to Him, "What sign do You show to us, since You do these things?"

19 Jesus answered and said to them, "Destroy this temple, and in three days I will raise it up."

20 Then the Jews said, "It has taken forty-six years to build this temple, and will You raise it up in three days?"

21 But He was speaking of the temple of His body.

22 Therefore, when He had risen from the dead, His disciples remembered that He had said this to them; and they believed the Scripture and the word which Jesus had said.

23 Now when He was in Jerusalem at the Passover, during the feast, many believed in His name when they saw the signs which He did.

24 But Jesus did not commit Himself to them, because He knew all men,

25 and had no need that anyone should testify of man, for He knew what was in man.

Promise to Claim: _____
_____
_____
Something to Enrich my Life: _____
_____
_____
Something to Change: _____
_____
_____

3 There was a man of the Pharisees named Nicodemus, a ruler of the Jews.

2 This man came to Jesus by night and said to Him, "Rabbi, we know that You are a teacher come from God; for no one can do these signs that You do unless God is with him."

3 Jesus answered and said to him, "Most assuredly, I say to you, unless one is born again, he cannot see the kingdom of God."

4 Nicodemus said to Him, "How can a man be born when

he is old? Can he enter a second time into his mother's womb and be born?"

5 Jesus answered, "Most assuredly, I say to you, unless one is born of water and the Spirit, he cannot enter the kingdom of God.

6 "That which is born of the flesh is flesh, and that which is born of the Spirit is spirit.

7 "Do not marvel that I said to you, 'You must be born again.'

8 "The wind blows where it wishes, and you hear the sound of it, but cannot tell where it comes from and where it goes. So is everyone who is born of the Spirit."

9 Nicodemus answered and said to Him, "How can these things be?"

10 Jesus answered and said to him, "Are you the teacher of Israel, and do not know these things?

11 "Most assuredly, I say to you, We speak what We know and testify what We have seen, and you do not receive Our witness.

12 "If I have told you earthly things and you do not believe, how will you believe if I tell you heavenly things?

13 "No one has ascended to heaven but He who came down from heaven, that is, the Son of Man who is in heaven.

14 "And as Moses lifted up the serpent in the wilderness, even so must the Son of Man be lifted up,

15 "that whoever believes in Him should not perish but have eternal life.

16 "For God so loved the world that He gave His only begotten Son, that whoever believes in Him should not perish but have everlasting life.

17 "For God did not send His Son into the world to condemn the world, but that the world through Him might be saved.

18 "He who believes in Him is not condemned; but he who does not believe is condemned already, because he has not believed in the name of the only begotten Son of God.

19 "And this is the condemnation, that the light has come into the world, and men loved darkness rather than light, because their deeds were evil.

20 "For everyone practicing evil hates the light and does not come to the light, lest his deeds should be exposed.

21 "But he who does the truth comes to the light, that his deeds may be clearly seen, that they have been done in God."

22 After these things Jesus and His disciples came into the land of Judea, and there He remained with them and baptized.

23 Now John also was baptizing in Aenon near Salim, because there was much water there. And they came and were baptized.

24 For John had not yet been thrown into prison.

25 Then there arose a dispute between some of John's disciples and the Jews about purification.

26 And they came to John and said to him, "Rabbi, He who was with you beyond the Jordan, to whom you have testified; behold, He is baptizing, and all are coming to Him!"

27 John answered and said, "A man can receive nothing unless it has been given to him from heaven.

28 "You yourselves bear me witness, that I said, 'I am not the Christ,' but, 'I have been sent before Him.'

29 "He who has the bride is the bridegroom; but the friend of the bridegroom, who stands and hears him, rejoices greatly because of the bridegroom's voice. Therefore this joy of mine is fulfilled.

30 "He must increase, but I must decrease.

31 "He who comes from above is above all; he who is of the earth is earthly and speaks of the earth. He who comes from heaven is above all.

32 "And what He has seen and heard, that He testifies; and no one receives His testimony.

33 "He who has received His testimony has certified that God is true.

34 "For He whom God has sent speaks the words of God, for God does not give the Spirit by measure.

35 "The Father loves the Son, and has given all things into His hand.

36 "He who believes in the Son has everlasting life; and he who does not believe the Son shall not see life, but the wrath of God abides on him."

Promise to Claim: _____
_____
_____
Something to Enrich my Life:_____
_____
_____
Something to Change: _____
_____
_____

4 Therefore, when the Lord knew that the Pharisees had heard that Jesus made and baptized more disciples than John

2 (though Jesus Himself did not baptize, but His disciples),

3 He left Judea and departed again to Galilee.

4 But He needed to go through Samaria.

5 So He came to a city of Samaria which is called Sychar, near the plot of ground that Jacob gave to his son Joseph.

6 Now Jacob's well was there. Jesus therefore, being wearied from His journey, sat thus by the well. It was about the sixth hour.

7 A woman of Samaria came to draw water. Jesus said to her, "Give Me a drink."

8 For His disciples had gone away into the city to buy food.

9 Then the woman of Samaria said to Him, "How is it that You, being a Jew, ask a drink from me, a Samaritan woman?" For Jews have no dealings with Samaritans.

10 Jesus answered and said to her, "If you knew the gift of God, and who it is who says to you, 'Give Me a drink,' you would have asked Him, and He would have given you living water."

11 The woman said to Him, "Sir, You have nothing to draw with, and the well is deep. Where then do You get that living water?

12 "Are You greater than our father Jacob, who gave us the well, and drank from it himself, as well as his sons and his livestock?"

13 Jesus answered and said to her, "Whoever drinks of this water will thirst again,

14 "but whoever drinks of the water that I shall give him will never thirst. But the water that I shall give him will become in him a fountain of water springing up into everlasting life."

15 The woman said to Him, "Sir, give me this water, that I may not thirst, nor come here to draw."

16 Jesus said to her, "Go, call your husband, and come here."

17 The woman answered and said, "I have no husband." Jesus said to her, "You have well said, 'I have no husband,'

18 "for you have had five husbands, and the one whom you now have is not your husband; in that you spoke truly."

19 The woman said to Him, "Sir, I perceive that You are a prophet.

20 "Our fathers worshiped

on this mountain, and you Jews say that in Jerusalem is the place where one ought to worship."

21 Jesus said to her, "Woman, believe Me, the hour is coming when you will neither on this mountain, nor in Jerusalem, worship the Father.

22 "You worship what you do not know; we know what we worship, for salvation is of the Jews.

23 "But the hour is coming, and now is, when the true worshipers will worship the Father in spirit and truth; for the Father is seeking such to worship Him.

24 "God is Spirit, and those who worship Him must worship in spirit and truth."

25 The woman said to Him, "I know that Messiah is coming" (who is called Christ). "When He comes, He will tell us all things."

26 Jesus said to her, "I who speak to you am He."

27 And at this point His disciples came, and they marveled that He talked with a woman; yet no one said, "What do You seek?" or, "Why are You talking with her?"

28 The woman then left her waterpot, went her way into the city, and said to the men,

29 "Come, see a Man who told me all things that I ever did. Could this be the Christ?"

30 Then they went out of the city and came to Him.

31 In the meantime His disciples urged Him, saying, "Rabbi, eat."

32 But He said to them, "I have food to eat of which you do not know."

33 Therefore the disciples said to one another, "Has anyone brought Him anything to eat?"

34 Jesus said to them, "My food is to do the will of Him who sent Me, and to finish His work.

35 "Do you not say, 'There are still four months and then comes the harvest'? Behold, I say to you, lift up your eyes and look at the fields, for they are already white for harvest!

36 "And he who reaps receives wages, and gathers fruit for eternal life, that both he who sows and he who reaps may rejoice together.

37 "For in this the saying is true: 'One sows and another reaps.'

38 "I sent you to reap that for which you have not labored; others have labored, and you

have entered into their labors."

39 And many of the Samaritans of that city believed in Him because of the word of the woman who testified, "He told me all that I ever did."

40 So when the Samaritans had come to Him, they urged Him to stay with them; and He stayed there two days.

41 And many more believed because of His own word.

42 Then they said to the woman, "Now we believe, not because of what you said, for we ourselves have heard Him and we know that this is indeed the Christ, the Savior of the world."

43 Now after the two days He departed from there and went to Galilee.

44 For Jesus Himself testified that a prophet has no honor in his own country.

45 So when He came to Galilee, the Galileans received Him, having seen all the things He did in Jerusalem at the feast; for they also had gone to the feast.

46 So Jesus came again to Cana of Galilee where He had made the water wine. And there was a certain nobleman whose son was sick at Capernaum.

47 When he heard that Jesus had come out of Judea into Galilee, he went to Him and implored Him to come down and heal his son, for he was at the point of death.

48 Then Jesus said to him, "Unless you people see signs and wonders, you will by no means believe."

49 The nobleman said to Him, "Sir, come down before my child dies!"

50 Jesus said to him, "Go your way; your son lives." So the man believed the word that Jesus spoke to him, and he went his way.

51 And as he was now going down, his servants met him and told him, saying, "Your son lives!"

52 Then he inquired of them the hour when he got better. And they said to him, "Yesterday at the seventh hour the fever left him."

53 So the father knew that it was at the same hour in which Jesus said to him, "Your son lives." And he himself believed, and his whole household.

54 This again is the second sign Jesus did when He had come out of Judea into Galilee.

Promise to Claim: _____

_____

_____

Something to Enrich my Life:_____

_____

_____

Something to Change: _____

_____

_____

5 After this there was a feast of the Jews, and Jesus went up to Jerusalem.

2 Now there is in Jerusalem by the Sheep Gate a pool, which is called in Hebrew, Bethesda, having five porches.

3 In these lay a great multitude of sick people, blind, lame, paralyzed, waiting for the moving of the water.

4 For an angel went down at a certain time into the pool and stirred up the water; then whoever stepped in first, after the stirring of the water, was made well of whatever disease he had.

5 Now a certain man was there who had an infirmity thirty-eight years.

6 When Jesus saw him lying there, and knew that he already had been in that condition a long time, He said to him, "Do you want to be made well?"

7 The sick man answered Him, "Sir, I have no man to put me into the pool when the water is stirred up; but while I am coming, another steps down before me."

8 Jesus said to him, "Rise, take up your bed and walk."

9 And immediately the man was made well, took up his bed, and walked. And that day was the Sabbath.

10 The Jews therefore said to him who was cured, "It is the Sabbath; it is not lawful for you to carry your bed."

11 He answered them, "He who made me well said to me, 'Take up your bed and walk.'"

12 Then they asked him, "Who is the Man who said to you, 'Take up your bed and walk'?"

13 But the one who was healed did not know who it was, for Jesus had withdrawn, a multitude being in that place.

14 Afterward Jesus found him in the temple, and said to him, "See, you have been made well. Sin no more, lest a worse thing come upon you."

15 The man departed and told the Jews that it was Jesus who had made him well.

16 For this reason the Jews persecuted Jesus, and sought to kill Him, because He had done

these things on the Sabbath.

17 But Jesus answered them, "My Father has been working until now, and I have been working."

18 Therefore the Jews sought all the more to kill Him, because He not only broke the Sabbath, but also said that God was His Father, making Himself equal with God.

19 Then Jesus answered and said to them, "Most assuredly, I say to you, the Son can do nothing of Himself, but what He sees the Father do; for whatever He does, the Son also does in like manner.

20 "For the Father loves the Son, and shows Him all things that He Himself does; and He will show Him greater works than these, that you may marvel.

21 "For as the Father raises the dead and gives life to them, even so the Son gives life to whom He will.

22 "For the Father judges no one, but has committed all judgment to the Son,

23 "that all should honor the Son just as they honor the Father. He who does not honor the Son does not honor the Father who sent Him.

24 "Most assuredly, I say to you, he who hears My word and believes in Him who sent Me has everlasting life, and shall not come into judgment, but has passed from death into life.

25 "Most assuredly, I say to you, the hour is coming, and now is, when the dead will hear the voice of the Son of God; and those who hear will live.

26 "For as the Father has life in Himself, so He has granted the Son to have life in Himself,

27 "and has given Him authority to execute judgment also, because He is the Son of Man.

28 "Do not marvel at this; for the hour is coming in which all who are in the graves will hear His voice

29 "and come forth; those who have done good, to the resurrection of life, and those who have done evil, to the resurrection of condemnation.

30 "I can of Myself do nothing. As I hear, I judge; and My judgment is righteous, because I do not seek My own will but the will of the Father who sent Me.

31 "If I bear witness of Myself, My witness is not true.

32 "There is another who bears witness of Me, and I know that

the witness which He witnesses of Me is true.

33 "You have sent to John, and he has borne witness to the truth.

34 "Yet I do not receive testimony from man, but I say these things that you may be saved.

35 "He was the burning and shining lamp, and you were willing for a time to rejoice in his light.

36 "But I have a greater witness than John's; for the works which the Father has given Me to finish; the very works that I do; bear witness of Me, that the Father has sent Me.

37 "And the Father Himself, who sent Me, has testified of Me. You have neither heard His voice at any time, nor seen His form.

38 "But you do not have His word abiding in you, because whom He sent, Him you do not believe.

39 "You search the Scriptures, for in them you think you have eternal life; and these are they which testify of Me.

40 "But you are not willing to come to Me that you may have life.

41 "I do not receive honor from men.

42 "But I know you, that you do not have the love of God in you.

43 "I have come in My Father's name, and you do not receive Me; if another comes in his own name, him you will receive.

44 "How can you believe, who receive honor from one another, and do not seek the honor that comes from the only God?

45 "Do not think that I shall accuse you to the Father; there is one who accuses you; Moses, in whom you trust.

46 "For if you believed Moses, you would believe Me; for he wrote about Me.

47 "But if you do not believe his writings, how will you believe My words?"

Promise to Claim: _____
_____
_____
*Something to Enrich my Life:*_____
_____
_____
Something to Change: _____
_____
_____

6 After these things Jesus went over the Sea of Galilee,

which is the Sea of Tiberias.

2 Then a great multitude followed Him, because they saw His signs which He performed on those who were diseased.

3 And Jesus went up on the mountain, and there He sat with His disciples.

4 Now the Passover, a feast of the Jews, was near.

5 Then Jesus lifted up His eyes, and seeing a great multitude coming toward Him, He said to Philip, "Where shall we buy bread, that these may eat?"

6 But this He said to test him, for He Himself knew what He would do.

7 Philip answered Him, "Two hundred denarii worth of bread is not sufficient for them, that every one of them may have a little."

8 One of His disciples, Andrew, Simon Peter's brother, said to Him,

9 "There is a lad here who has five barley loaves and two small fish, but what are they among so many?"

10 Then Jesus said, "Make the people sit down." Now there was much grass in the place. So the men sat down, in number about five thousand.

11 And Jesus took the loaves, and when He had given thanks He distributed them to the disciples, and the disciples to those sitting down; and likewise of the fish, as much as they wanted.

12 So when they were filled, He said to His disciples, "Gather up the fragments that remain, so that nothing is lost."

13 Therefore they gathered them up, and filled twelve baskets with the fragments of the five barley loaves which were left over by those who had eaten.

14 Then those men, when they had seen the sign that Jesus did, said, "This is truly the Prophet who is to come into the world."

15 Therefore when Jesus perceived that they were about to come and take Him by force to make Him king, He departed again to the mountain by Himself alone.

16 Now when evening came, His disciples went down to the sea,

17 got into the boat, and went over the sea toward Capernaum. And it was already dark, and Jesus had not come to them.

18 Then the sea arose because a great wind was blowing.

19 So when they had rowed about three or four miles, they

saw Jesus walking on the sea and drawing near the boat; and they were afraid.

20 But He said to them, "It is I; do not be afraid."

21 Then they willingly received Him into the boat, and immediately the boat was at the land where they were going.

22 On the following day, when the people who were standing on the other side of the sea saw that there was no other boat there, except that one which His disciples had entered, and that Jesus had not entered the boat with His disciples, but His disciples had gone away alone;

23 however, other boats came from Tiberias, near the place where they ate bread after the Lord had given thanks;

24 when the people therefore saw that Jesus was not there, nor His disciples, they also got into boats and came to Capernaum, seeking Jesus.

25 And when they found Him on the other side of the sea, they said to Him, "Rabbi, when did You come here?"

26 Jesus answered them and said, "Most assuredly, I say to you, you seek Me, not because you saw the signs, but because you ate of the loaves and were filled.

27 "Do not labor for the food which perishes, but for the food which endures to everlasting life, which the Son of Man will give you, because God the Father has set His seal on Him."

28 Then they said to Him, "What shall we do, that we may work the works of God?"

29 Jesus answered and said to them, "This is the work of God, that you believe in Him whom He sent."

30 Therefore they said to Him, "What sign will You perform then, that we may see it and believe You? What work will You do?

31 "Our fathers ate the manna in the desert; as it is written, 'He gave them bread from heaven to eat.'"

32 Then Jesus said to them, "Most assuredly, I say to you, Moses did not give you the bread from heaven, but My Father gives you the true bread from heaven.

33 "For the bread of God is He who comes down from heaven and gives life to the world."

34 Then they said to Him, "Lord, give us this bread always."

35 And Jesus said to them, "I am the bread of life. He who comes to Me shall never

hunger, and he who believes in Me shall never thirst.

36 "But I said to you that you have seen Me and yet do not believe.

37 "All that the Father gives Me will come to Me, and the one who comes to Me I will by no means cast out.

38 "For I have come down from heaven, not to do My own will, but the will of Him who sent Me.

39 "This is the will of the Father who sent Me, that of all He has given Me I should lose nothing, but should raise it up at the last day.

40 "And this is the will of Him who sent Me, that everyone who sees the Son and believes in Him may have everlasting life; and I will raise him up at the last day."

41 The Jews then complained about Him, because He said, "I am the bread which came down from heaven."

42 And they said, "Is not this Jesus, the son of Joseph, whose father and mother we know? How is it then that He says, 'I have come down from heaven'?"

43 Jesus therefore answered and said to them, "Do not murmur among yourselves.

44 "No one can come to Me unless the Father who sent Me draws him; and I will raise him up at the last day.

45 "It is written in the prophets, 'And they shall all be taught by God.' Therefore everyone who has heard and learned from the Father comes to Me.

46 "Not that anyone has seen the Father, except He who is from God; He has seen the Father.

47 "Most assuredly, I say to you, he who believes in Me has everlasting life.

48 "I am the bread of life.

49 "Your fathers ate the manna in the wilderness, and are dead.

50 "This is the bread which comes down from heaven, that one may eat of it and not die.

51 "I am the living bread which came down from heaven. If anyone eats of this bread, he will live forever; and the bread that I shall give is My flesh, which I shall give for the life of the world."

52 The Jews therefore quarreled among themselves, saying, "How can this Man give us His flesh to eat?"

53 Then Jesus said to them, "Most assuredly, I say to you, unless you eat the flesh of the

Son of Man and drink His blood, you have no life in you.

54 "Whoever eats My flesh and drinks My blood has eternal life, and I will raise him up at the last day.

55 "For My flesh is food indeed, and My blood is drink indeed.

56 "He who eats My flesh and drinks My blood abides in Me, and I in him.

57 "As the living Father sent Me, and I live because of the Father, so he who feeds on Me will live because of Me.

58 "This is the bread which came down from heaven; not as your fathers ate the manna, and are dead. He who eats this bread will live forever."

59 These things He said in the synagogue as He taught in Capernaum.

60 Therefore many of His disciples, when they heard this, said, "This is a hard saying; who can understand it?"

61 When Jesus knew in Himself that His disciples complained about this, He said to them, "Does this offend you?

62 "What then if you should see the Son of Man ascend where He was before?

63 "It is the Spirit who gives life; the flesh profits nothing. The words that I speak to you are spirit, and they are life.

64 "But there are some of you who do not believe." For Jesus knew from the beginning who they were who did not believe, and who would betray Him.

65 And He said, "Therefore I have said to you that no one can come to Me unless it has been granted to him by My Father."

66 From that time many of His disciples went back and walked with Him no more.

67 Then Jesus said to the twelve, "Do you also want to go away?"

68 But Simon Peter answered Him, "Lord, to whom shall we go? You have the words of eternal life.

69 "Also we have come to believe and know that You are the Christ, the Son of the living God."

70 Jesus answered them, "Did I not choose you, the twelve, and one of you is a devil?"

71 He spoke of Judas Iscariot, the son of Simon, for it was he who would betray Him, being one of the twelve.

Promise to Claim: _____

_____

_____

*Something to Enrich my Life:*_____

_____

_____

Something to Change: _____

_____

_____

7 After these things Jesus walked in Galilee; for He did not want to walk in Judea, because the Jews sought to kill Him.

2 Now the Jews' Feast of Tabernacles was at hand.

3 His brothers therefore said to Him, "Depart from here and go into Judea, that Your disciples also may see the works that You are doing.

4 "For no one does anything in secret while he himself seeks to be known openly. If You do these things, show Yourself to the world."

5 For even His brothers did not believe in Him.

6 Then Jesus said to them, "My time has not yet come, but your time is always ready.

7 "The world cannot hate you, but it hates Me because I testify of it that its works are evil.

8 "You go up to this feast. I am not yet going up to this feast, for My time has not yet fully come."

9 When He had said these things to them, He remained in Galilee.

10 But when His brothers had gone up, then He also went up to the feast, not openly, but as it were in secret.

11 Then the Jews sought Him at the feast, and said, "Where is He?"

12 And there was much complaining among the people concerning Him. Some said, "He is good"; others said, "No, on the contrary, He deceives the people."

13 However, no one spoke openly of Him for fear of the Jews.

14 Now about the middle of the feast Jesus went up into the temple and taught.

15 And the Jews marveled, saying, "How does this Man know letters, having never studied?"

16 Jesus answered them and said, "My doctrine is not Mine, but His who sent Me.

17 "If anyone wants to do His will, he shall know concerning the doctrine, whether it is from God or whether I speak on My own authority.

18 "He who speaks from himself seeks his own glory; but He

who seeks the glory of the One who sent Him is true, and no unrighteousness is in Him.

19 "Did not Moses give you the law, yet none of you keeps the law? Why do you seek to kill Me?"

20 The people answered and said, "You have a demon. Who is seeking to kill You?"

21 Jesus answered and said to them, "I did one work, and you all marvel.

22 "Moses therefore gave you circumcision (not that it is from Moses, but from the fathers), and you circumcise a man on the Sabbath.

23 "If a man receives circumcision on the Sabbath, so that the law of Moses should not be broken, are you angry with Me because I made a man completely well on the Sabbath?

24 "Do not judge according to appearance, but judge with righteous judgment."

25 Now some of them from Jerusalem said, "Is this not He whom they seek to kill?

26 "But look! He speaks boldly, and they say nothing to Him. Do the rulers know indeed that this is truly the Christ?

27 "However, we know where this Man is from; but when the Christ comes, no one knows where He is from."

28 Then Jesus cried out, as He taught in the temple, saying, "You both know Me, and you know where I am from; and I have not come of Myself, but He who sent Me is true, whom you do not know.

29 "But I know Him, for I am from Him, and He sent Me."

30 Therefore they sought to take Him; but no one laid a hand on Him, because His hour had not yet come.

31 And many of the people believed in Him, and said, "When the Christ comes, will He do more signs than these which this Man has done?"

32 The Pharisees heard the crowd murmuring these things concerning Him, and the Pharisees and the chief priests sent officers to take Him.

33 Then Jesus said to them, "I shall be with you a little while longer, and then I go to Him who sent Me.

34 "You will seek Me and not find Me, and where I am you cannot come."

35 Then the Jews said among themselves, "Where does He intend to go that we shall not find Him? Does He intend to go to the Dispersion among the Greeks and teach the Greeks?

36 "What is this thing that He said, 'You will seek Me and not find Me, and where I am you cannot come'?"

37 On the last day, that great day of the feast, Jesus stood and cried out, saying, "If anyone thirsts, let him come to Me and drink.

38 "He who believes in Me, as the Scripture has said, out of his heart will flow rivers of living water."

39 But this He spoke concerning the Spirit, whom those believing in Him would receive; for the Holy Spirit was not yet given, because Jesus was not yet glorified.

40 Therefore many from the crowd, when they heard this saying, said, "Truly this is the Prophet."

41 Others said, "This is the Christ." But some said, "Will the Christ come out of Galilee?

42 "Has not the Scripture said that the Christ comes from the seed of David and from the town of Bethlehem, where David was?"

43 So there was a division among the people because of Him.

44 Now some of them wanted to take Him, but no one laid hands on Him.

45 Then the officers came to the chief priests and Pharisees, who said to them, "Why have you not brought Him?"

46 The officers answered, "No man ever spoke like this Man!"

47 Then the Pharisees answered them, "Are you also deceived?

48 "Have any of the rulers or the Pharisees believed in Him?

49 "But this crowd that does not know the law is accursed."

50 Nicodemus (he who came to Jesus by night, being one of them) said to them,

51 "Does our law judge a man before it hears him and knows what he is doing?"

52 They answered and said to him, "Are you also from Galilee? Search and look, for no prophet has arisen out of Galilee."

53 And everyone went to his own house.

Promise to Claim: _____

_____

_____

*Something to Enrich my Life:*_____

_____

_____

Something to Change: _____

_____

_____

8 But Jesus went to the Mount of Olives.

2 Now early in the morning He came again into the temple, and all the people came to Him; and He sat down and taught them.

3 Then the scribes and Pharisees brought to Him a woman caught in adultery. And when they had set her in the midst,

4 they said to Him, "Teacher, this woman was caught in adultery, in the very act.

5 "Now Moses, in the law, commanded us that such should be stoned. But what do You say?"

6 This they said, testing Him, that they might have something of which to accuse Him. But Jesus stooped down and wrote on the ground with His finger, as though He did not hear.

7 So when they continued asking Him, He raised Himself up and said to them, "He who is without sin among you, let him throw a stone at her first."

8 And again He stooped down and wrote on the ground.

9 Then those who heard it, being convicted by their conscience, went out one by one, beginning with the oldest even to the last. And Jesus was left alone, and the woman standing in the midst.

10 When Jesus had raised Himself up and saw no one but the woman, He said to her, "Woman, where are those accusers of yours? Has no one condemned you?"

11 She said, "No one, Lord." And Jesus said to her, "Neither do I condemn you; go and sin no more."

12 Then Jesus spoke to them again, saying, "I am the light of the world. He who follows Me shall not walk in darkness, but have the light of life."

13 The Pharisees therefore said to Him, "You bear witness of Yourself; Your witness is not true."

14 Jesus answered and said to them, "Even if I bear witness of Myself, My witness is true, for I know where I came from and where I am going; but you do not know where I come from and where I am going.

15 "You judge according to the flesh; I judge no one.

16 "And yet if I do judge, My judgment is true; for I am not alone, but I am with the Father who sent Me.

17 "It is also written in your

law that the testimony of two men is true.

18 "I am One who bears witness of Myself, and the Father who sent Me bears witness of Me."

19 Then they said to Him, "Where is Your Father?" Jesus answered, "You know neither Me nor My Father. If you had known Me, you would have known My Father also."

20 These words Jesus spoke in the treasury, as He taught in the temple; and no one laid hands on Him, for His hour had not yet come.

21 Then Jesus said to them again, "I am going away, and you will seek Me, and will die in your sin. Where I go you cannot come."

22 So the Jews said, "Will He kill Himself, because He says, 'Where I go you cannot come'?"

23 And He said to them, "You are from beneath; I am from above. You are of this world; I am not of this world.

24 "Therefore I said to you that you will die in your sins; for if you do not believe that I am He, you will die in your sins."

25 Then they said to Him, "Who are You?" And Jesus said to them, "Just what I have been saying to you from the beginning.

26 "I have many things to say and to judge concerning you, but He who sent Me is true; and I speak to the world those things which I heard from Him."

27 They did not understand that He spoke to them of the Father.

28 Then Jesus said to them, "When you lift up the Son of Man, then you will know that I am He, and that I do nothing of Myself; but as My Father taught Me, I speak these things.

29 "And He who sent Me is with Me. The Father has not left Me alone, for I always do those things that please Him."

30 As He spoke these words, many believed in Him.

31 Then Jesus said to those Jews who believed Him, "If you abide in My word, you are My disciples indeed.

32 "And you shall know the truth, and the truth shall make you free."

33 They answered Him, "We are Abraham's descendants, and have never been in bondage to anyone. How can you say, 'You will be made free'?"

34 Jesus answered them,

"Most assuredly, I say to you, whoever commits sin is a slave of sin.

35 "And a slave does not abide in the house forever, but a son abides forever.

36 "Therefore if the Son makes you free, you shall be free indeed.

37 "I know that you are Abraham's descendants, but you seek to kill Me, because My word has no place in you.

38 "I speak what I have seen with My Father, and you do what you have seen with your father."

39 They answered and said to Him, "Abraham is our father." Jesus said to them, "If you were Abraham's children, you would do the works of Abraham.

40 "But now you seek to kill Me, a Man who has told you the truth which I heard from God. Abraham did not do this.

41 "You do the deeds of your father." Then they said to Him, "We were not born of fornication; we have one Father; God."

42 Jesus said to them, "If God were your Father, you would love Me, for I proceeded forth and came from God; nor have I come of Myself, but He sent Me.

43 "Why do you not understand My speech? Because you are not able to listen to My word.

44 "You are of your father the devil, and the desires of your father you want to do. He was a murderer from the beginning, and does not stand in the truth, because there is no truth in him. When he speaks a lie, he speaks from his own resources, for he is a liar and the father of it.

45 "But because I tell the truth, you do not believe Me.

46 "Which of you convicts Me of sin? And if I tell the truth, why do you not believe Me?

47 "He who is of God hears God's words; therefore you do not hear, because you are not of God."

48 Then the Jews answered and said to Him, "Do we not say rightly that You are a Samaritan and have a demon?"

49 Jesus answered, "I do not have a demon; but I honor My Father, and you dishonor Me.

50 "And I do not seek My own glory; there is One who seeks and judges.

51 "Most assuredly, I say to you, if anyone keeps My word he shall never see death."

52 Then the Jews said to Him, "Now we know that You have a

demon! Abraham is dead, and the prophets; and You say, 'If anyone keeps My word he shall never taste death.'

53 "Are You greater than our father Abraham, who is dead? And the prophets are dead. Whom do You make Yourself out to be?"

54 Jesus answered, "If I honor Myself, My honor is nothing. It is My Father who honors Me, of whom you say that He is your God.

55 "Yet you have not known Him, but I know Him. And if I say, 'I do not know Him,' I shall be a liar like you; but I do know Him and keep His word.

56 "Your father Abraham rejoiced to see My day, and he saw it and was glad."

57 Then the Jews said to Him, "You are not yet fifty years old, and have You seen Abraham?"

58 Jesus said to them, "Most assuredly, I say to you, before Abraham was, I AM."

59 Then they took up stones to throw at Him; but Jesus hid Himself and went out of the temple, going through the midst of them, and so passed by.

Promise to Claim: _____
_____
_____
Something to Enrich my Life:_____
_____
_____
Something to Change: _____
_____
_____

9 Now as Jesus passed by, He saw a man who was blind from birth.

2 And His disciples asked Him, saying, "Rabbi, who sinned, this man or his parents, that he was born blind?"

3 Jesus answered, "Neither this man nor his parents sinned, but that the works of God should be revealed in him.

4 "I must work the works of Him who sent Me while it is day; the night is coming when no one can work.

5 "As long as I am in the world, I am the light of the world."

6 When He had said these things, He spat on the ground and made clay with the saliva; and He anointed the eyes of the blind man with the clay.

7 And He said to him, "Go, wash in the pool of Siloam" (which is translated, Sent). So he went and washed, and came

back seeing.

8 Therefore the neighbors and those who previously had seen that he was blind said, "Is not this he who sat and begged?"

9 Some said, "This is he." Others said, "He is like him." He said, "I am he."

10 Therefore they said to him, "How were your eyes opened?"

11 He answered and said, "A Man called Jesus made clay and anointed my eyes and said to me, 'Go to the pool of Siloam and wash.' So I went and washed, and I received sight."

12 Then they said to him, "Where is He?" He said, "I do not know."

13 They brought him who formerly was blind to the Pharisees.

14 Now it was a Sabbath when Jesus made the clay and opened his eyes.

15 Then the Pharisees also asked him again how he had received his sight. He said to them, "He put clay on my eyes, and I washed, and I see."

16 Therefore some of the Pharisees said, "This Man is not from God, because He does not keep the Sabbath." Others said, "How can a man who is a sinner do such signs?" And there was a division among them.

17 They said to the blind man again, "What do you say about Him because He opened your eyes?" He said, "He is a prophet."

18 But the Jews did not believe concerning him, that he had been blind and received his sight, until they called the parents of him who had received his sight.

19 And they asked them, saying, "Is this your son, who you say was born blind? How then does he now see?"

20 His parents answered them and said, "We know that this is our son, and that he was born blind;

21 "but by what means he now sees we do not know, or who opened his eyes we do not know. He is of age; ask him. He will speak for himself."

22 His parents said these things because they feared the Jews, for the Jews had agreed already that if anyone confessed that He was Christ, he would be put out of the synagogue.

23 Therefore his parents said, "He is of age; ask him."

24 So they again called the man who was blind, and said to him, "Give God the glory! We know that this Man is a sinner."

25 He answered and said,

"Whether He is a sinner or not I do not know. One thing I know: that though I was blind, now I see."

26 Then they said to him again, "What did He do to you? How did He open your eyes?"

27 He answered them, "I told you already, and you did not listen. Why do you want to hear it again? Do you also want to become His disciples?"

28 Then they reviled him and said, "You are His disciple, but we are Moses' disciples.

29 "We know that God spoke to Moses; as for this fellow, we do not know where He is from."

30 The man answered and said to them, "Why, this is a marvelous thing, that you do not know where He is from; yet He has opened my eyes!

31 "Now we know that God does not hear sinners; but if anyone is a worshiper of God and does His will, He hears him.

32 "Since the world began it has been unheard of that anyone opened the eyes of one who was born blind.

33 "If this Man were not from God, He could do nothing."

34 They answered and said to him, "You were completely born in sins, and are you teaching us?" And they cast him out.

35 Jesus heard that they had cast him out; and when He had found him, He said to him, "Do you believe in the Son of God?"

36 He answered and said, "Who is He, Lord, that I may believe in Him?"

37 And Jesus said to him, "You have both seen Him and it is He who is talking with you."

38 Then he said, "Lord, I believe!" And he worshiped Him.

39 And Jesus said, "For judgment I have come into this world, that those who do not see may see, and that those who see may be made blind."

40 Then some of the Pharisees who were with Him heard these words, and said to Him, "Are we blind also?"

41 Jesus said to them, "If you were blind, you would have no sin; but now you say, 'We see.' Therefore your sin remains.

Promise to Claim: _____

_____

_____

Something to Enrich my Life:_____

_____

_____

Something to Change: _____

_____

_____

10 "Most assuredly, I say to you, he who does not enter the sheepfold by the door, but climbs up some other way, the same is a thief and a robber.

2 "But he who enters by the door is the shepherd of the sheep.

3 "To him the doorkeeper opens, and the sheep hear his voice; and he calls his own sheep by name and leads them out.

4 "And when he brings out his own sheep, he goes before them; and the sheep follow him, for they know his voice.

5 "Yet they will by no means follow a stranger, but will flee from him, for they do not know the voice of strangers."

6 Jesus used this illustration, but they did not understand the things which He spoke to them.

7 Then Jesus said to them again, "Most assuredly, I say to you, I am the door of the sheep.

8 "All who ever came before Me are thieves and robbers, but the sheep did not hear them.

9 "I am the door. If anyone enters by Me, he will be saved, and will go in and out and find pasture.

10 "The thief does not come except to steal, and to kill, and to destroy. I have come that they may have life, and that they may have it more abundantly.

11 "I am the good shepherd. The good shepherd gives His life for the sheep.

12 "But a hireling, he who is not the shepherd, one who does not own the sheep, sees the wolf coming and leaves the sheep and flees; and the wolf catches the sheep and scatters them.

13 "The hireling flees because he is a hireling and does not care about the sheep.

14 "I am the good shepherd; and I know My sheep, and am known by My own.

15 "As the Father knows Me, even so I know the Father; and I lay down My life for the sheep.

16 "And other sheep I have which are not of this fold; them also I must bring, and they will hear My voice; and there will be one flock and one shepherd.

17 "Therefore My Father loves Me, because I lay down My life that I may take it again.

18 "No one takes it from Me, but I lay it down of Myself. I have power to lay it down, and I have power to take it again.

This command I have received from My Father."

19 Therefore there was a division again among the Jews because of these sayings.

20 And many of them said, "He has a demon and is mad. Why do you listen to Him?"

21 Others said, "These are not the words of one who has a demon. Can a demon open the eyes of the blind?"

22 Now it was the Feast of Dedication in Jerusalem, and it was winter.

23 And Jesus walked in the temple, in Solomon's porch.

24 Then the Jews surrounded Him and said to Him, "How long do You keep us in doubt? If You are the Christ, tell us plainly."

25 Jesus answered them, "I told you, and you do not believe. The works that I do in My Father's name, they bear witness of Me.

26 "But you do not believe, because you are not of My sheep, as I said to you.

27 "My sheep hear My voice, and I know them, and they follow Me.

28 "And I give them eternal life, and they shall never perish; neither shall anyone snatch them out of My hand.

29 "My Father, who has given them to Me, is greater than all; and no one is able to snatch them out of My Father's hand.

30 "I and My Father are one."

31 Then the Jews took up stones again to stone Him.

32 Jesus answered them, "Many good works I have shown you from My Father. For which of those works do you stone Me?"

33 The Jews answered Him, saying, "For a good work we do not stone You, but for blasphemy, and because You, being a Man, make Yourself God."

34 Jesus answered them, "Is it not written in your law, 'I said, "You are gods"'?

35 "If He called them gods, to whom the word of God came (and the Scripture cannot be broken),

36 "do you say of Him whom the Father sanctified and sent into the world, 'You are blaspheming,' because I said, 'I am the Son of God'?

37 "If I do not do the works of My Father, do not believe Me;

38 "but if I do, though you do not believe Me, believe the works, that you may know and believe that the Father is in Me, and I in Him."

39 Therefore they sought

again to seize Him, but He escaped out of their hand.

40 And He went away again beyond the Jordan to the place where John was baptizing at first, and there He stayed.

41 Then many came to Him and said, "John performed no sign, but all the things that John spoke about this Man were true."

42 And many believed in Him there.

Promise to Claim: _____
_____
_____
Something to Enrich my Life: _____
_____
_____
Something to Change: _____
_____
_____

11 Now a certain man was sick, Lazarus of Bethany, the town of Mary and her sister Martha.

2 It was that Mary who anointed the Lord with fragrant oil and wiped His feet with her hair, whose brother Lazarus was sick.

3 Therefore the sisters sent to Him, saying, "Lord, behold, he whom You love is sick."

4 When Jesus heard that, He said, "This sickness is not unto death, but for the glory of God, that the Son of God may be glorified through it."

5 Now Jesus loved Martha and her sister and Lazarus.

6 So, when He heard that he was sick, He stayed two more days in the place where He was.

7 Then after this He said to the disciples, "Let us go to Judea again."

8 The disciples said to Him, "Rabbi, lately the Jews sought to stone You, and are You going there again?"

9 Jesus answered, "Are there not twelve hours in the day? If anyone walks in the day, he does not stumble, because he sees the light of this world.

10 "But if one walks in the night, he stumbles, because the light is not in him."

11 These things He said, and after that He said to them, "Our friend Lazarus sleeps, but I go that I may wake him up."

12 Then His disciples said, "Lord, if he sleeps he will get well."

13 However, Jesus spoke of his death, but they thought that He was speaking about taking rest in sleep.

14 Then Jesus said to them plainly, "Lazarus is dead.

15 "And I am glad for your sakes that I was not there, that you may believe. Nevertheless let us go to him."

16 Then Thomas, who is called the Twin, said to his fellow disciples, "Let us also go, that we may die with Him."

17 So when Jesus came, He found that he had already been in the tomb four days.

18 Now Bethany was near Jerusalem, about two miles away.

19 And many of the Jews had joined the women around Martha and Mary, to comfort them concerning their brother.

20 Then Martha, as soon as she heard that Jesus was coming, went and met Him, but Mary was sitting in the house.

21 Then Martha said to Jesus, "Lord, if You had been here, my brother would not have died.

22 "But even now I know that whatever You ask of God, God will give You."

23 Jesus said to her, "Your brother will rise again."

24 Martha said to Him, "I know that he will rise again in the resurrection at the last day."

25 Jesus said to her, "I am the resurrection and the life. He who believes in Me, though he may die, he shall live.

26 "And whoever lives and believes in Me shall never die. Do you believe this?"

27 She said to Him, "Yes, Lord, I believe that You are the Christ, the Son of God, who is to come into the world."

28 And when she had said these things, she went her way and secretly called Mary her sister, saying, "The Teacher has come and is calling for you."

29 As soon as she heard that, she arose quickly and came to Him.

30 Now Jesus had not yet come into the town, but was in the place where Martha met Him.

31 Then the Jews who were with her in the house, and comforting her, when they saw that Mary rose up quickly and went out, followed her, saying, "She is going to the tomb to weep there."

32 Then, when Mary came where Jesus was, and saw Him, she fell down at His feet, saying to Him, "Lord, if You had been here, my brother would not have died."

33 Therefore, when Jesus saw her weeping, and the Jews who

came with her weeping, He groaned in the spirit and was troubled.

34 And He said, "Where have you laid him?" They said to Him, "Lord, come and see."

35 Jesus wept.

36 Then the Jews said, "See how He loved him!"

37 And some of them said, "Could not this Man, who opened the eyes of the blind, also have kept this man from dying?"

38 Then Jesus, again groaning in Himself, came to the tomb. It was a cave, and a stone lay against it.

39 Jesus said, "Take away the stone." Martha, the sister of him who was dead, said to Him, "Lord, by this time there is a stench, for he has been dead four days."

40 Jesus said to her, "Did I not say to you that if you would believe you would see the glory of God?"

41 Then they took away the stone from the place where the dead man was lying. And Jesus lifted up His eyes and said, "Father, I thank You that You have heard Me.

42 "And I know that You always hear Me, but because of the people who are standing by I said this, that they may believe that You sent Me."

43 Now when He had said these things, He cried with a loud voice, "Lazarus, come forth!"

44 And he who had died came out bound hand and foot with graveclothes, and his face was wrapped with a cloth. Jesus said to them, "Loose him, and let him go."

45 Then many of the Jews who had come to Mary, and had seen the things Jesus did, believed in Him.

46 But some of them went away to the Pharisees and told them the things Jesus did.

47 Then the chief priests and the Pharisees gathered a council and said, "What shall we do? For this Man works many signs.

48 "If we let Him alone like this, everyone will believe in Him, and the Romans will come and take away both our place and nation."

49 And one of them, Caiaphas, being high priest that year, said to them, "You know nothing at all,

50 "nor do you consider that it is expedient for us that one man should die for the people, and not that the whole nation should perish."

51 Now this he did not say on his own authority; but being high priest that year he prophesied that Jesus would die for the nation,

52 and not for that nation only, but also that He would gather together in one the children of God who were scattered abroad.

53 Then, from that day on, they plotted to put Him to death.

54 Therefore Jesus no longer walked openly among the Jews, but went from there into the country near the wilderness, to a city called Ephraim, and there remained with His disciples.

55 And the Passover of the Jews was near, and many went from the country up to Jerusalem before the Passover, to purify themselves.

56 Then they sought Jesus, and spoke among themselves as they stood in the temple, "What do you think; that He will not come to the feast?"

57 Now both the chief priests and the Pharisees had given a command, that if anyone knew where He was, he should report it, that they might seize Him.

Promise to Claim: _____
_____
_____
Something to Enrich my Life:_____
_____
_____
Something to Change: _____
_____
_____

12 Then, six days before the Passover, Jesus came to Bethany, where Lazarus was who had been dead, whom He had raised from the dead.

2 There they made Him a supper; and Martha served, but Lazarus was one of those who sat at the table with Him.

3 Then Mary took a pound of very costly oil of spikenard, anointed the feet of Jesus, and wiped His feet with her hair. And the house was filled with the fragrance of the oil.

4 Then one of His disciples, Judas Iscariot, Simon's son, who would betray Him, said,

5 "Why was this fragrant oil not sold for three hundred denarii and given to the poor?"

6 This he said, not that he cared for the poor, but because he was a thief, and had the money box; and he used to take what was put in it.

7 But Jesus said, "Let her alone; she has kept this for the day of My burial.

8 "For the poor you have with you always, but Me you do not have always."

9 Now a great many of the Jews knew that He was there; and they came, not for Jesus' sake only, but that they might also see Lazarus, whom He had raised from the dead.

10 But the chief priests plotted to put Lazarus to death also,

11 because on account of him many of the Jews went away and believed in Jesus.

12 The next day a great multitude that had come to the feast, when they heard that Jesus was coming to Jerusalem,

13 took branches of palm trees and went out to meet Him, and cried out: "Hosanna! 'Blessed is He who comes in the name of the LORD!' The King of Israel!"

14 Then Jesus, when He had found a young donkey, sat on it; as it is written:

15 "Fear not, daughter of Zion; Behold, your King is coming, Sitting on a donkey's colt."

16 His disciples did not understand these things at first; but when Jesus was glorified, then they remembered that these things were written about Him and that they had done these things to Him.

17 Therefore the people, who were with Him when He called Lazarus out of his tomb and raised him from the dead, bore witness.

18 For this reason the people also met Him, because they heard that He had done this sign.

19 The Pharisees therefore said among themselves, "You see that you are accomplishing nothing. Look, the world has gone after Him!"

20 Now there were certain Greeks among those who came up to worship at the feast.

21 Then they came to Philip, who was from Bethsaida of Galilee, and asked him, saying, "Sir, we wish to see Jesus."

22 Philip came and told Andrew, and in turn Andrew and Philip told Jesus.

23 But Jesus answered them, saying, "The hour has come that the Son of Man should be glorified.

24 "Most assuredly, I say to you, unless a grain of wheat falls into the ground and dies, it remains alone; but if it dies, it produces much grain.

25 "He who loves his life will

lose it, and he who hates his life in this world will keep it for eternal life.

26 "If anyone serves Me, let him follow Me; and where I am, there My servant will be also. If anyone serves Me, him My Father will honor.

27 "Now My soul is troubled, and what shall I say? 'Father, save Me from this hour'? But for this purpose I came to this hour.

28 "Father, glorify Your name." Then a voice came from heaven, saying, "I have both glorified it and will glorify it again."

29 Therefore the people who stood by and heard it said that it had thundered. Others said, "An angel has spoken to Him."

30 Jesus answered and said, "This voice did not come because of Me, but for your sake.

31 "Now is the judgment of this world; now the ruler of this world will be cast out.

32 "And I, if I am lifted up from the earth, will draw all peoples to Myself."

33 This He said, signifying by what death He would die.

34 The people answered Him, "We have heard from the law that the Christ remains forever; and how can You say, 'The Son of Man must be lifted up'? Who is this Son of Man?"

35 Then Jesus said to them, "A little while longer the light is with you. Walk while you have the light, lest darkness overtake you; he who walks in darkness does not know where he is going.

36 "While you have the light, believe in the light, that you may become sons of light." These things Jesus spoke, and departed, and was hidden from them.

37 But although He had done so many signs before them, they did not believe in Him,

38 that the word of Isaiah the prophet might be fulfilled, which he spoke: "Lord, who has believed our report? And to whom has the arm of the LORD been revealed?"

39 Therefore they could not believe, because Isaiah said again:

40 "He has blinded their eyes and hardened their hearts, Lest they should see with their eyes, Lest they should understand with their hearts and turn, So that I should heal them."

41 These things Isaiah said when he saw His glory and spoke of Him.

42 Nevertheless even among the rulers many believed

in Him, but because of the Pharisees they did not confess Him, lest they should be put out of the synagogue;

43 for they loved the praise of men more than the praise of God.

44 Then Jesus cried out and said, "He who believes in Me, believes not in Me but in Him who sent Me.

45 "And he who sees Me sees Him who sent Me.

46 "I have come as a light into the world, that whoever believes in Me should not abide in darkness.

47 "And if anyone hears My words and does not believe, I do not judge him; for I did not come to judge the world but to save the world.

48 "He who rejects Me, and does not receive My words, has that which judges him; the word that I have spoken will judge him in the last day.

49 "For I have not spoken on My own authority; but the Father who sent Me gave Me a command, what I should say and what I should speak.

50 "And I know that His command is everlasting life. Therefore, whatever I speak, just as the Father has told Me, so I speak."

Promise to Claim: _____
_____
_____
Something to Enrich my Life: _____
_____
_____
Something to Change: _____
_____
_____

13 Now before the feast of the Passover, when Jesus knew that His hour had come that He should depart from this world to the Father, having loved His own who were in the world, He loved them to the end.

2 And supper being ended, the devil having already put it into the heart of Judas Iscariot, Simon's son, to betray Him,

3 Jesus, knowing that the Father had given all things into His hands, and that He had come from God and was going to God,

4 rose from supper and laid aside His garments, took a towel and girded Himself.

5 After that, He poured water into a basin and began to wash the disciples' feet, and to wipe them with the towel with

which He was girded.

6 Then He came to Simon Peter. And Peter said to Him, "Lord, are You washing my feet?"

7 Jesus answered and said to him, "What I am doing you do not understand now, but you will know after this."

8 Peter said to Him, "You shall never wash my feet!" Jesus answered him, "If I do not wash you, you have no part with Me."

9 Simon Peter said to Him, "Lord, not my feet only, but also my hands and my head!"

10 Jesus said to him, "He who is bathed needs only to wash his feet, but is completely clean; and you are clean, but not all of you."

11 For He knew who would betray Him; therefore He said, "You are not all clean."

12 So when He had washed their feet, taken His garments, and sat down again, He said to them, "Do you know what I have done to you?

13 "You call me Teacher and Lord, and you say well, for so I am.

14 "If I then, your Lord and Teacher, have washed your feet, you also ought to wash one another's feet.

15 "For I have given you an example, that you should do as I have done to you.

16 "Most assuredly, I say to you, a servant is not greater than his master; nor is he who is sent greater than he who sent him.

17 "If you know these things, blessed are you if you do them.

18 "I do not speak concerning all of you. I know whom I have chosen; but that the Scripture may be fulfilled, 'He who eats bread with Me has lifted up his heel against Me.'

19 "Now I tell you before it comes, that when it does come to pass, you may believe that I am He.

20 "Most assuredly, I say to you, he who receives whomever I send receives Me; and he who receives Me receives Him who sent Me."

21 When Jesus had said these things, He was troubled in spirit, and testified and said, "Most assuredly, I say to you, one of you will betray Me."

22 Then the disciples looked at one another, perplexed about whom He spoke.

23 Now there was leaning on Jesus' bosom one of His disciples, whom Jesus loved.

24 Simon Peter therefore motioned to him to ask who it was of whom He spoke.

25 Then, leaning back on Jesus' breast, he said to Him, "Lord, who is it?"

26 Jesus answered, "It is he to whom I shall give a piece of bread when I have dipped it." And having dipped the bread, He gave it to Judas Iscariot, the son of Simon.

27 Now after the piece of bread, Satan entered him. Then Jesus said to him, "What you do, do quickly."

28 But no one at the table knew for what reason He said this to him.

29 For some thought, because Judas had the money box, that Jesus had said to him, "Buy those things we need for the feast," or that he should give something to the poor.

30 Having received the piece of bread, he then went out immediately. And it was night.

31 So, when he had gone out, Jesus said, "Now the Son of Man is glorified, and God is glorified in Him.

32 "If God is glorified in Him, God will also glorify Him in Himself, and glorify Him immediately.

33 "Little children, I shall be with you a little while longer. You will seek Me; and as I said to the Jews, 'Where I am going,

you cannot come,' so now I say to you.

34 "A new commandment I give to you, that you love one another; as I have loved you, that you also love one another.

35 "By this all will know that you are My disciples, if you have love for one another."

36 Simon Peter said to Him, "Lord, where are You going?" Jesus answered him, "Where I am going you cannot follow Me now, but you shall follow Me afterward."

37 Peter said to Him, "Lord, why can I not follow You now? I will lay down my life for Your sake."

38 Jesus answered him, "Will you lay down your life for My sake? Most assuredly, I say to you, the rooster shall not crow till you have denied Me three times.

Promise to Claim: _____

_____

_____

Something to Enrich my Life: _____

_____

_____

Something to Change: _____

_____

_____

14 "Let not your heart be troubled; you believe in God, believe also in Me.

2 "In My Father's house are many mansions; if it were not so, I would have told you. I go to prepare a place for you.

3 "And if I go and prepare a place for you, I will come again and receive you to Myself; that where I am, there you may be also.

4 "And where I go you know, and the way you know."

5 Thomas said to Him, "Lord, we do not know where You are going, and how can we know the way?"

6 Jesus said to him, "I am the way, the truth, and the life. No one comes to the Father except through Me.

7 "If you had known Me, you would have known My Father also; and from now on you know Him and have seen Him."

8 Philip said to Him, "Lord, show us the Father, and it is sufficient for us."

9 Jesus said to him, "Have I been with you so long, and yet you have not known Me, Philip? He who has seen Me has seen the Father; so how can you say, 'Show us the Father'?

10 "Do you not believe that I am in the Father, and the Father in Me? The words that I speak to you I do not speak on My own authority; but the Father who dwells in Me does the works.

11 "Believe Me that I am in the Father and the Father in Me, or else believe Me for the sake of the works themselves.

12 "Most assuredly, I say to you, he who believes in Me, the works that I do he will do also; and greater works than these he will do, because I go to My Father.

13 "And whatever you ask in My name, that I will do, that the Father may be glorified in the Son.

14 "If you ask anything in My name, I will do it.

15 "If you love Me, keep My commandments.

16 "And I will pray the Father, and He will give you another Helper, that He may abide with you forever;

17 "the Spirit of truth, whom the world cannot receive, because it neither sees Him nor knows Him; but you know Him, for He dwells with you and will be in you.

18 "I will not leave you orphans; I will come to you.

19 "A little while longer and the world will see Me no more, but you will see Me. Because I live, you will live also.

20 "At that day you will know that I am in My Father, and you in Me, and I in you.

21 "He who has My commandments and keeps them, it is he who loves Me. And he who loves Me will be loved by My Father, and I will love him and manifest Myself to him."

22 Judas (not Iscariot) said to Him, "Lord, how is it that You will manifest Yourself to us, and not to the world?"

23 Jesus answered and said to him, "If anyone loves Me, he will keep My word; and My Father will love him, and We will come to him and make Our home with him.

24 "He who does not love Me does not keep My words; and the word which you hear is not Mine but the Father's who sent Me.

25 "These things I have spoken to you while being present with you.

26 "But the Helper, the Holy Spirit, whom the Father will send in My name, He will teach you all things, and bring to your remembrance all things that I said to you.

27 "Peace I leave with you, My peace I give to you; not as the world gives do I give to you. Let not your heart be troubled, neither let it be afraid.

28 "You have heard Me say to you, 'I am going away and coming back to you.' If you loved Me, you would rejoice because I said, 'I am going to the Father,' for My Father is greater than I.

29 "And now I have told you before it comes, that when it does come to pass, you may believe.

30 "I will no longer talk much with you, for the ruler of this world is coming, and he has nothing in Me.

31 "But that the world may know that I love the Father, and as the Father gave Me commandment, so I do. Arise, let us go from here.

Promise to Claim: _____

_____

_____

Something to Enrich my Life: _____

_____

_____

Something to Change: _____

_____

_____

15 "I am the true vine, and My Father is the vinedresser.

2 "Every branch in Me that does not bear fruit He takes away; and every branch that bears fruit He prunes, that it may bear more fruit.

3 "You are already clean because of the word which I have spoken to you.

4 "Abide in Me, and I in you. As the branch cannot bear fruit of itself, unless it abides in the vine, neither can you, unless you abide in Me.

5 "I am the vine, you are the branches. He who abides in Me, and I in him, bears much fruit; for without Me you can do nothing.

6 "If anyone does not abide in Me, he is cast out as a branch and is withered; and they gather them and throw them into the fire, and they are burned.

7 "If you abide in Me, and My words abide in you, you will ask what you desire, and it shall be done for you.

8 "By this My Father is glorified, that you bear much fruit; so you will be My disciples.

9 "As the Father loved Me, I also have loved you; abide in My love.

10 "If you keep My commandments, you will abide in My love, just as I have kept My Father's commandments and abide in His love.

11 "These things I have spoken to you, that My joy may remain in you, and that your joy may be full.

12 "This is My commandment, that you love one another as I have loved you.

13 "Greater love has no one than this, than to lay down one's life for his friends.

14 "You are My friends if you do whatever I command you.

15 "No longer do I call you servants, for a servant does not know what his master is doing; but I have called you friends, for all things that I heard from My Father I have made known to you.

16 "You did not choose Me, but I chose you and appointed you that you should go and bear fruit, and that your fruit should remain, that whatever you ask the Father in My name He may give you.

17 "These things I command you, that you love one another.

18 "If the world hates you, you know that it hated Me before it hated you.

19 "If you were of the world, the world would love its own. Yet because you are not of the

world, but I chose you out of the world, therefore the world hates you.

20 "Remember the word that I said to you, 'A servant is not greater than his master.' If they persecuted Me, they will also persecute you. If they kept My word, they will keep yours also.

21 "But all these things they will do to you for My name's sake, because they do not know Him who sent Me.

22 "If I had not come and spoken to them, they would have no sin, but now they have no excuse for their sin.

23 "He who hates Me hates My Father also.

24 "If I had not done among them the works which no one else did, they would have no sin; but now they have seen and also hated both Me and My Father.

25 "But this happened that the word might be fulfilled which is written in their law, 'They hated Me without a cause.'

26 "But when the Helper comes, whom I shall send to you from the Father, the Spirit of truth who proceeds from the Father, He will testify of Me.

27 "And you also will bear witness, because you have been with Me from the beginning.

Promise to Claim: _____
_____
_____

*Something to Enrich my Life:*_____
_____
_____

Something to Change: _____
_____
_____

16 "These things I have spoken to you, that you should not be made to stumble.

2 "They will put you out of the synagogues; yes, the time is coming that whoever kills you will think that he offers God service.

3 "And these things they will do to you because they have not known the Father nor Me.

4 "But these things I have told you, that when the time comes, you may remember that I told you of them. And these things I did not say to you at the beginning, because I was with you.

5 "But now I go away to Him who sent Me, and none of you asks Me, 'Where are You going?'

6 "But because I have said

these things to you, sorrow has filled your heart.

7 "Nevertheless I tell you the truth. It is to your advantage that I go away; for if I do not go away, the Helper will not come to you; but if I depart, I will send Him to you.

8 "And when He has come, He will convict the world of sin, and of righteousness, and of judgment:

9 "of sin, because they do not believe in Me;

10 "of righteousness, because I go to My Father and you see Me no more;

11 "of judgment, because the ruler of this world is judged.

12 "I still have many things to say to you, but you cannot bear them now.

13 "However, when He, the Spirit of truth, has come, He will guide you into all truth; for He will not speak on His own authority, but whatever He hears He will speak; and He will tell you things to come.

14 "He will glorify Me, for He will take of what is Mine and declare it to you.

15 "All things that the Father has are Mine. Therefore I said that He will take of Mine and declare it to you.

16 "A little while, and you will not see Me; and again a little while, and you will see Me, because I go to the Father."

17 Then some of His disciples said among themselves, "What is this that He says to us, 'A little while, and you will not see Me; and again a little while, and you will see Me'; and, 'because I go to the Father'?"

18 They said therefore, "What is this that He says, 'A little while'? We do not know what He is saying."

19 Now Jesus knew that they desired to ask Him, and He said to them, "Are you inquiring among yourselves about what I said, 'A little while, and you will not see Me; and again a little while, and you will see Me'?

20 "Most assuredly, I say to you that you will weep and lament, but the world will rejoice; and you will be sorrowful, but your sorrow will be turned into joy.

21 "A woman, when she is in labor, has sorrow because her hour has come; but as soon as she has given birth to the child, she no longer remembers the anguish, for joy that a human being has been born into the world.

22 "Therefore you now have sorrow; but I will see you again and your heart will rejoice, and your joy no one will take from you.

23 "And in that day you will ask Me nothing. Most assuredly, I say to you, whatever you ask the Father in My name He will give you.

24 "Until now you have asked nothing in My name. Ask, and you will receive, that your joy may be full.

25 "These things I have spoken to you in figurative language; but the time is coming when I will no longer speak to you in figurative language, but I will tell you plainly about the Father.

26 "In that day you will ask in My name, and I do not say to you that I shall pray the Father for you;

27 "for the Father Himself loves you, because you have loved Me, and have believed that I came forth from God.

28 "I came forth from the Father and have come into the world. Again, I leave the world and go to the Father."

29 His disciples said to Him, "See, now You are speaking plainly, and using no figure of speech!

30 "Now we are sure that You know all things, and have no need that anyone should question You. By this we believe that You came forth from God."

31 Jesus answered them, "Do you now believe?

32 "Indeed the hour is coming, yes, has now come, that you will be scattered, each to his own, and will leave Me alone. And yet I am not alone, because the Father is with Me.

33 "These things I have spoken to you, that in Me you may have peace. In the world you will have tribulation; but be of good cheer, I have overcome the world."

Promise to Claim: _____
_____
_____
Something to Enrich my Life: _____
_____
_____
Something to Change: _____
_____
_____

17 Jesus spoke these words, lifted up His eyes to heaven, and said: "Father, the hour has come. Glorify Your Son, that Your Son also may glorify You,

2 "as You have given Him authority over all flesh, that He should give eternal life to as many as You have given Him.

3 "And this is eternal life, that they may know You, the only true God, and Jesus Christ whom You have sent.

4 "I have glorified You on the earth. I have finished the work which You have given Me to do.

5 "And now, O Father, glorify Me together with Yourself, with the glory which I had with You before the world was.

6 "I have manifested Your name to the men whom You have given Me out of the world. They were Yours, You gave them to Me, and they have kept Your word.

7 "Now they have known that all things which You have given Me are from You.

8 "For I have given to them the words which You have given Me; and they have received them, and have known surely that I came forth from You; and they have believed that You sent Me.

9 "I pray for them. I do not pray for the world but for those whom You have given Me, for they are Yours.

10 "And all Mine are Yours, and Yours are Mine, and I am glorified in them.

11 "Now I am no longer in the world, but these are in the world, and I come to You. Holy Father, keep through Your name those whom You have given Me, that they may be one as We are.

12 "While I was with them in the world, I kept them in Your name. Those whom You gave Me I have kept; and none of them is lost except the son of perdition, that the Scripture might be fulfilled.

13 "But now I come to You, and these things I speak in the world, that they may have My joy fulfilled in themselves.

14 "I have given them Your word; and the world has hated them because they are not of the world, just as I am not of the world.

15 "I do not pray that You should take them out of the world, but that You should keep them from the evil one.

16 "They are not of the world, just as I am not of the world.

17 "Sanctify them by Your truth. Your word is truth.

18 "As You sent Me into the world, I also have sent them into the world.

19 "And for their sakes I

sanctify Myself, that they also may be sanctified by the truth.

20 "I do not pray for these alone, but also for those who will believe in Me through their word;

21 "that they all may be one, as You, Father, are in Me, and I in You; that they also may be one in Us, that the world may believe that You sent Me.

22 "And the glory which You gave Me I have given them, that they may be one just as We are one:

23 "I in them, and You in Me; that they may be made perfect in one, and that the world may know that You have sent Me, and have loved them as You have loved Me.

24 "Father, I desire that they also whom You gave Me may be with Me where I am, that they may behold My glory which You have given Me; for You loved Me before the foundation of the world.

25 "O righteous Father! The world has not known You, but I have known You; and these have known that You sent Me.

26 "And I have declared to them Your name, and will declare it, that the love with which You loved Me may be in them, and I in them."

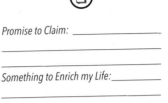

Promise to Claim: _____
_____
_____
Something to Enrich my Life:_____
_____
_____
Something to Change: _____
_____
_____

18 When Jesus had spoken these words, He went out with His disciples over the Brook Kidron, where there was a garden, which He and His disciples entered.

2 And Judas, who betrayed Him, also knew the place; for Jesus often met there with His disciples.

3 Then Judas, having received a detachment of troops, and officers from the chief priests and Pharisees, came there with lanterns, torches, and weapons.

4 Jesus therefore, knowing all things that would come upon Him, went forward and said to them, "Whom are you seeking?"

5 They answered Him, "Jesus of Nazareth." Jesus said to them, "I am He." And Judas,

who betrayed Him, also stood with them.

6 Now when He said to them, "I am He," they drew back and fell to the ground.

7 Then He asked them again, "Whom are you seeking?" And they said, "Jesus of Nazareth."

8 Jesus answered, "I have told you that I am He. Therefore, if you seek Me, let these go their way,"

9 that the saying might be fulfilled which He spoke, "Of those whom You gave Me I have lost none."

10 Then Simon Peter, having a sword, drew it and struck the high priest's servant, and cut off his right ear. The servant's name was Malchus.

11 So Jesus said to Peter, "Put your sword into the sheath. Shall I not drink the cup which My Father has given Me?"

12 Then the detachment of troops and the captain and the officers of the Jews arrested Jesus and bound Him.

13 And they led Him away to Annas first, for he was the father-in-law of Caiaphas who was high priest that year.

14 Now it was Caiaphas who advised the Jews that it was expedient that one man should die for the people.

15 And Simon Peter followed Jesus, and so did another disciple. Now that disciple was known to the high priest, and went with Jesus into the courtyard of the high priest.

16 But Peter stood at the door outside. Then the other disciple, who was known to the high priest, went out and spoke to her who kept the door, and brought Peter in.

17 Then the servant girl who kept the door said to Peter, "You are not also one of this Man's disciples, are you?" He said, "I am not."

18 Now the servants and officers who had made a fire of coals stood there, for it was cold, and they warmed themselves. And Peter stood with them and warmed himself.

19 The high priest then asked Jesus about His disciples and His doctrine.

20 Jesus answered him, "I spoke openly to the world. I always taught in synagogues and in the temple, where the Jews always meet, and in secret I have said nothing.

21 "Why do you ask Me? Ask those who have heard Me what I said to them. Indeed they know what I said."

22 And when He had said

these things, one of the officers who stood by struck Jesus with the palm of his hand, saying, "Do You answer the high priest like that?"

23 Jesus answered him, "If I have spoken evil, bear witness of the evil; but if well, why do you strike Me?"

24 Then Annas sent Him bound to Caiaphas the high priest.

25 Now Simon Peter stood and warmed himself. Therefore they said to him, "You are not also one of His disciples, are you?" He denied it and said, "I am not!"

26 One of the servants of the high priest, a relative of him whose ear Peter cut off, said, "Did I not see you in the garden with Him?"

27 Peter then denied again; and immediately a rooster crowed.

28 Then they led Jesus from Caiaphas to the Praetorium, and it was early morning. But they themselves did not go into the Praetorium, lest they should be defiled, but that they might eat the Passover.

29 Pilate then went out to them and said, "What accusation do you bring against this Man?"

30 They answered and said to him, "If He were not an evildoer, we would not have delivered Him up to you."

31 Then Pilate said to them, "You take Him and judge Him according to your law." Therefore the Jews said to him, "It is not lawful for us to put anyone to death,"

32 that the saying of Jesus might be fulfilled which He spoke, signifying by what death He would die.

33 Then Pilate entered the Praetorium again, called Jesus, and said to Him, "Are You the King of the Jews?"

34 Jesus answered him, "Are you speaking for yourself about this, or did others tell you this concerning Me?"

35 Pilate answered, "Am I a Jew? Your own nation and the chief priests have delivered You to me. What have You done?"

36 Jesus answered, "My kingdom is not of this world. If My kingdom were of this world, My servants would fight, so that I should not be delivered to the Jews; but now My kingdom is not from here."

37 Pilate therefore said to Him, "Are You a king then?" Jesus answered, "You say rightly that I am a king. For this cause

I was born, and for this cause I have come into the world, that I should bear witness to the truth. Everyone who is of the truth hears My voice."

38 Pilate said to Him, "What is truth?" And when he had said this, he went out again to the Jews, and said to them, "I find no fault in Him at all.

39 "But you have a custom that I should release someone to you at the Passover. Do you therefore want me to release to you the King of the Jews?"

40 Then they all cried again, saying, "Not this Man, but Barabbas!" Now Barabbas was a robber.

Promise to Claim: _____
_____
_____

Something to Enrich my Life:_____
_____
_____

Something to Change: _____
_____
_____

19 So then Pilate took Jesus and scourged Him.

2 And the soldiers twisted a crown of thorns and put it on His head, and they put on Him a purple robe.

3 Then they said, "Hail, King of the Jews!" And they struck Him with their hands.

4 Pilate then went out again, and said to them, "Behold, I am bringing Him out to you, that you may know that I find no fault in Him."

5 Then Jesus came out, wearing the crown of thorns and the purple robe. And Pilate said to them, "Behold the Man!"

6 Therefore, when the chief priests and officers saw Him, they cried out, saying, "Crucify Him, crucify Him!" Pilate said to them, "You take Him and crucify Him, for I find no fault in Him."

7 The Jews answered him, "We have a law, and according to our law He ought to die, because He made Himself the Son of God."

8 Therefore, when Pilate heard that saying, he was the more afraid,

9 and went again into the Praetorium, and said to Jesus, "Where are You from?" But Jesus gave him no answer.

10 Then Pilate said to Him, "Are You not speaking to me? Do You not know that I have power to crucify You, and

power to release You?"

11 Jesus answered, "You could have no power at all against Me unless it had been given you from above. Therefore the one who delivered Me to you has the greater sin."

12 From then on Pilate sought to release Him, but the Jews cried out, saying, "If you let this Man go, you are not Caesar's friend. Whoever makes himself a king speaks against Caesar."

13 When Pilate therefore heard that saying, he brought Jesus out and sat down in the judgment seat in a place that is called The Pavement, but in Hebrew, Gabbatha.

14 Now it was the Preparation Day of the Passover, and about the sixth hour. And he said to the Jews, "Behold your King!"

15 But they cried out, "Away with Him, away with Him! Crucify Him!" Pilate said to them, "Shall I crucify your King?" The chief priests answered, "We have no king but Caesar!"

16 Then he delivered Him to them to be crucified. So they took Jesus and led Him away.

17 And He, bearing His cross, went out to a place called the Place of a Skull, which is called in Hebrew, Golgotha,

18 where they crucified Him, and two others with Him, one on either side, and Jesus in the center.

19 Now Pilate wrote a title and put it on the cross. And the writing was: JESUS OF NAZARETH, THE KING OF THE JEWS.

20 Then many of the Jews read this title, for the place where Jesus was crucified was near the city; and it was written in Hebrew, Greek, and Latin.

21 Therefore the chief priests of the Jews said to Pilate, "Do not write, 'The King of the Jews,' but, 'He said, "I am the King of the Jews."' "

22 Pilate answered, "What I have written, I have written."

23 Then the soldiers, when they had crucified Jesus, took His garments and made four parts, to each soldier a part, and also the tunic. Now the tunic was without seam, woven from the top in one piece.

24 They said therefore among themselves, "Let us not tear it, but cast lots for it, whose it shall be," that the Scripture might be fulfilled which says: "They divided My garments among them, And for My clothing they cast lots." Therefore the soldiers did these things.

25 Now there stood by the cross of Jesus His mother, and His mother's sister, Mary the wife of Clopas, and Mary Magdalene.

26 When Jesus therefore saw His mother, and the disciple whom He loved standing by, He said to His mother, "Woman, behold your son!"

27 Then He said to the disciple, "Behold your mother!" And from that hour that disciple took her to his own home.

28 After this, Jesus, knowing that all things were now accomplished, that the Scripture might be fulfilled, said, "I thirst!"

29 Now a vessel full of sour wine was sitting there; and they filled a sponge with sour wine, put it on hyssop, and put it to His mouth.

30 So when Jesus had received the sour wine, He said, "It is finished!" And bowing His head, He gave up His spirit.

31 Therefore, because it was the Preparation Day, that the bodies should not remain on the cross on the Sabbath (for that Sabbath was a high day), the Jews asked Pilate that their legs might be broken, and that they might be taken away.

32 Then the soldiers came and broke the legs of the first and of the other who was crucified with Him.

33 But when they came to Jesus and saw that He was already dead, they did not break His legs.

34 But one of the soldiers pierced His side with a spear, and immediately blood and water came out.

35 And he who has seen has testified, and his testimony is true; and he knows that he is telling the truth, so that you may believe.

36 For these things were done that the Scripture should be fulfilled, "Not one of His bones shall be broken."

37 And again another Scripture says, "They shall look on Him whom they pierced."

38 After this, Joseph of Arimathea, being a disciple of Jesus, but secretly, for fear of the Jews, asked Pilate that he might take away the body of Jesus; and Pilate gave him permission. So he came and took the body of Jesus.

39 And Nicodemus, who at first came to Jesus by night, also came, bringing a mixture of myrrh and aloes, about a hundred pounds.

40 Then they took the body

of Jesus, and bound it in strips of linen with the spices, as the custom of the Jews is to bury.

41 Now in the place where He was crucified there was a garden, and in the garden a new tomb in which no one had yet been laid.

42 So there they laid Jesus, because of the Jews' Preparation Day, for the tomb was nearby.

Promise to Claim: _____

_____

_____

*Something to Enrich my Life:*_____

_____

_____

Something to Change: _____

_____

_____

20 Now on the first day of the week Mary Magdalene went to the tomb early, while it was still dark, and saw that the stone had been taken away from the tomb.

2 Then she ran and came to Simon Peter, and to the other disciple, whom Jesus loved, and said to them, "They have taken away the Lord out of the tomb, and we do not know where they have laid Him."

3 Peter therefore went out, and the other disciple, and were going to the tomb.

4 So they both ran together, and the other disciple outran Peter and came to the tomb first.

5 And he, stooping down and looking in, saw the linen cloths lying there; yet he did not go in.

6 Then Simon Peter came, following him, and went into the tomb; and he saw the linen cloths lying there,

7 and the handkerchief that had been around His head, not lying with the linen cloths, but folded together in a place by itself.

8 Then the other disciple, who came to the tomb first, went in also; and he saw and believed.

9 For as yet they did not know the Scripture, that He must rise again from the dead.

10 Then the disciples went away again to their own homes.

11 But Mary stood outside by the tomb weeping, and as she wept she stooped down and looked into the tomb.

12 And she saw two angels in white sitting, one at the head and the other at the feet, where the body of Jesus had lain.

13 Then they said to her, "Woman, why are you weeping?" She said to them, "Because they have taken away my Lord, and I do not know where they have laid Him."

14 Now when she had said this, she turned around and saw Jesus standing there, and did not know that it was Jesus.

15 Jesus said to her, "Woman, why are you weeping? Whom are you seeking?" She, supposing Him to be the gardener, said to Him, "Sir, if You have carried Him away, tell me where You have laid Him, and I will take Him away."

16 Jesus said to her, "Mary!" She turned and said to Him, "Rabboni!" (which is to say, Teacher).

17 Jesus said to her, "Do not cling to Me, for I have not yet ascended to My Father; but go to My brethren and say to them, 'I am ascending to My Father and your Father, and to My God and your God.'"

18 Mary Magdalene came and told the disciples that she had seen the Lord, and that He had spoken these things to her.

19 Then, the same day at evening, being the first day of the week, when the doors were shut where the disciples were assembled, for fear of the Jews, Jesus came and stood in the midst, and said to them, "Peace be with you."

20 When He had said this, He showed them His hands and His side. Then the disciples were glad when they saw the Lord.

21 So Jesus said to them again, "Peace to you! As the Father has sent Me, I also send you."

22 And when He had said this, He breathed on them, and said to them, "Receive the Holy Spirit.

23 "If you forgive the sins of any, they are forgiven them; if you retain the sins of any, they are retained."

24 Now Thomas, called the Twin, one of the twelve, was not with them when Jesus came.

25 The other disciples therefore said to him, "We have seen the Lord." So he said to them, "Unless I see in His hands the print of the nails, and put my finger into the print of the nails, and put my hand into His side, I will not believe."

26 And after eight days His disciples were again inside, and Thomas with them. Jesus came, the doors being shut, and stood

in the midst, and said, "Peace to you!"

27 Then He said to Thomas, "Reach your finger here, and look at My hands; and reach your hand here, and put it into My side. Do not be unbelieving, but believing."

28 And Thomas answered and said to Him, "My Lord and my God!"

29 Jesus said to him, "Thomas, because you have seen Me, you have believed. Blessed are those who have not seen and yet have believed."

30 And truly Jesus did many other signs in the presence of His disciples, which are not written in this book;

31 but these are written that you may believe that Jesus is the Christ, the Son of God, and that believing you may have life in His name.

Promise to Claim: _____
_____
_____

*Something to Enrich my Life:*_____
_____
_____

Something to Change: _____
_____
_____

21 After these things Jesus showed Himself again to the disciples at the Sea of Tiberias, and in this way He showed Himself:

2 Simon Peter, Thomas called the Twin, Nathanael of Cana in Galilee, the sons of Zebedee, and two others of His disciples were together.

3 Simon Peter said to them, "I am going fishing." They said to him, "We are going with you also." They went out and immediately got into the boat, and that night they caught nothing.

4 But when the morning had now come, Jesus stood on the shore; yet the disciples did not know that it was Jesus.

5 Then Jesus said to them, "Children, have you any food?" They answered Him, "No."

6 And He said to them, "Cast the net on the right side of the boat, and you will find some." So they cast, and now they were not able to draw it in because of the multitude of fish.

7 Therefore that disciple whom Jesus loved said to Peter, "It is the Lord!" Now when Simon Peter heard that it was the Lord, he put on his outer garment (for he had removed it), and plunged into the sea.

8 But the other disciples came in the little boat (for they were not far from land, but about two hundred cubits), dragging the net with fish.

9 Then, as soon as they had come to land, they saw a fire of coals there, and fish laid on it, and bread.

10 Jesus said to them, "Bring some of the fish which you have just caught."

11 Simon Peter went up and dragged the net to land, full of large fish, one hundred and fifty-three; and although there were so many, the net was not broken.

12 Jesus said to them, "Come and eat breakfast." Yet none of the disciples dared ask Him, "Who are You?"; knowing that it was the Lord.

13 Jesus then came and took the bread and gave it to them, and likewise the fish.

14 This is now the third time Jesus showed Himself to His disciples after He was raised from the dead.

15 So when they had eaten breakfast, Jesus said to Simon Peter, "Simon, son of Jonah, do you love Me more than these?" He said to Him, "Yes, Lord; You know that I love You." He said to him, "Feed My lambs."

16 He said to him again a second time, "Simon, son of Jonah, do you love Me?" He said to Him, "Yes, Lord; You know that I love You." He said to him, "Tend My sheep."

17 He said to him the third time, "Simon, son of Jonah, do you love Me?" Peter was grieved because He said to him the third time, "Do you love Me?" And he said to Him, "Lord, You know all things; You know that I love You." Jesus said to him, "Feed My sheep.

18 "Most assuredly, I say to you, when you were younger, you girded yourself and walked where you wished; but when you are old, you will stretch out your hands, and another will gird you and carry you where you do not wish."

19 This He spoke, signifying by what death he would glorify God. And when He had spoken this, He said to him, "Follow Me."

20 Then Peter, turning around, saw the disciple whom Jesus loved following, who also had leaned on His breast at the supper, and said, "Lord, who is the one who betrays You?"

21 Peter, seeing him, said to Jesus, "But Lord, what about this man?"

22 Jesus said to him, "If I will that he remain till I come, what is that to you? You follow Me."

23 Then this saying went out among the brethren that this disciple would not die. Yet Jesus did not say to him that he would not die, but, "If I will that he remain till I come, what is that to you?"

24 This is the disciple who testifies of these things, and wrote these things; and we know that his testimony is true.

25 And there are also many other things that Jesus did, which if they were written one by one, I suppose that even the world itself could not contain the books that would be written. Amen.

Promise to Claim: _____
_____
_____
Something to Enrich my Life:_____
_____
_____
Something to Change: _____
_____
_____

Congratulations!

You have just completed "Twenty-One Days with God." We hope that these have been enriching and enlightening times of study, prayer and fellowship with the Lord. If we can be of any help to you, answer your questions or suggest further resources, please feel free to contact us at:

Maranatha Chapel
10752 Coastwood Road
San Diego, CA 92127 USA
858 613 7800
email: office@maranathachapel.org

www.maranathachapel.org